BERKLEY BOOKS

New York

WHAT
TEACHERS
MAKE

IN PRAISE OF
THE GREATEST JOB
IN THE WORLD

Taylor Mali

THE BERKLEY PUBLISHING GROUP
Published by the Penguin Group
Penguin Group (USA)
375 Hudson Street, New York, New York 10014, USA

USA | Canada | UK | Ireland | Australia | New Zealand | India | South Africa | China

Penguin Books Ltd., Registered Offices: 80 Strand, London WC2R 0RL, England
For more information about the Penguin Group, visit penguin.com.

Copyright © 2012 by Taylor Mali

BERKLEY® is a registered trademark of Penguin Group (USA)
The "B" design is a trademark of Penguin Group (USA)

The Library of Congress has catalogued the G. P. Putnam's Sons hardcover edition as follows:

Mali, Taylor.
What teachers make : in praise of the greatest job in the world / Taylor Mali.
        p.   cm.
ISBN 978-0-399-15854-4
1. Teachers—Conduct of life.   2. Teaching.   3. Motivation in education.
I. Mali, Taylor. What teachers make.   II. Title.
LB1775. M4245   2012   2011050661
                371.1—dc23

PUBLISHING HISTORY
G. P. Putnam's Sons hardcover edition / March 2012
Berkley trade paperback edition / September 2013
ISBN: 978-0-425-26950-3

PRINTED IN THE UNITED STATES OF AMERICA
10   9   8   7

Cover design by Lisa Amoroso
Book design by Meighan Cavanaugh

All identifying names and characteristics have been changed
to protect the privacy of the individuals involved.

While the author has made every effort to provide accurate telephone numbers and Internet addresses at the time of publication, neither the author nor the publisher is responsible for errors, or for changes that occur after publication. Further, the publisher does not have any control over and does not assume any responsibility for author or third-party websites or their content.

ALWAYS LEARNING   PEARSON

Dedicated to Joe D'Angelo

Most of the fires I have lit came from your matches.

WHAT TEACHERS MAKE, OR
OBJECTION OVERRULED, OR
IF THINGS DON'T WORK OUT,
YOU CAN ALWAYS GO TO LAW SCHOOL

He says the problem with teachers is,
What's a kid going to learn from someone
who decided his best option in life was to become a teacher?
He reminds the other dinner guests that it's true
what they say about teachers:
Those who can, do; those who can't, teach.
I decide to bite my tongue—instead of his—
and resist the temptation to remind the other dinner
    guests
that it's also true what they say about lawyers.
Because we're eating, after all, and this is a polite
    conversation.

. . .

I mean, you're a teacher, Taylor.
Be honest. What do you make?

And I wish he hadn't done that—
asked me to be honest—
because, you see, I have a policy
about honesty and ass-kicking:
if you ask for it, I have to let you have it.
You want to know what I make?

I make kids work harder than they ever thought they
    could.
I can make a C+ feel like a Congressional Medal of
    Honor
and an A– feel like a slap in the face.
How dare you waste my time with anything less than your
    very best.

I make kids sit through 40 minutes of study hall
in absolute silence. *No, you may not work in groups.*
No, you may not ask a question.
Why won't I let you go to the bathroom?
Because you're bored.
And you don't really have to go to the bathroom, do you?

. . .

I make parents tremble in fear when I call home:
Hi. This is Mr. Mali. I hope I haven't called at a bad time,
I just wanted to talk to you about something your son said
    today.
To the biggest bully in the grade, he said, "Leave the kid alone.
I still cry sometimes, don't you? It's no big deal."
And it was the noblest act of courage I have ever seen.
I make parents see their children for who they are
and what they can be.

You want to know what I make?

I make kids wonder,
I make them question.
I make them criticize.
I make them apologize and mean it.
I make them write, write, write,
and then I make them read.
I make them spell
definitely beautiful, definitely beautiful,
definitely beautiful
over and over and over again until they will never misspell
either one of those words again.
I make them show all their work in math,

. . .

and hide it on their final drafts in English.
I make them understand that if you got *this*
then you follow *this*,
and if someone ever tries to judge you
by what you make, you give them *this*.

Here, let me break it down for you,
so you know what I say is true:
Teachers? Teachers make a difference!
Now what about you?

CONTENTS

WHAT
TEACHERS
MAKE

INTRODUCTION

This book exists because of a poem.

In 1997 I went to a New Year's Eve party where an arrogant young lawyer insulted me and the entire teaching profession. Teachers are so overworked and disrespected, he reasoned, that anyone who would choose to become a teacher today must be of questionable intelligence and therefore shouldn't really be allowed to teach in the first place. It was like something a mean-spirited Groucho Marx would say: anyone dumb enough to *want* to be a teacher shouldn't be allowed to be one. For the lawyer, it really came down to how poorly compensated teachers are—no intelligent person would take a job that paid less than what he was making as a lawyer. At the party that night I was so furious inside that I couldn't come up with a clever comeback, so I bit my tongue and laughed politely. But the next day, January 1, 1998, I wrote a poem that was the forceful response I wish I had delivered that night. The poem was called "What Teachers Make."

"What Teachers Make" wasn't published in a book until three years later, but I did post it immediately on my website, which like many websites back then was brand-new and had a lot of pages that said either "Under Construction" or "Coming Soon!" And shortly after I posted the poem, I started to get a lot of e-mails about it.

"What Teachers Make" struck a nerve; it is about defending teachers and why we teach, and our anger at being judged by the size of our paycheck instead of by the difference we make. The poem speaks to people, teachers and non-teachers alike. Unbeknownst to me, it was copied and pasted and e-mailed around the world, sometimes without my name attached to it, forwarded by friends with apologetic disclaimers about how they "don't normally forward things, but you must read this!"

The poem was excerpted by famous people giving speeches and delivering commencement addresses. Newspaper columnists wrote about the poem and quoted from it. Seattle Public Radio did a story about it. Other versions of the poem were written, either to clean up my language—I was angry when I wrote it, and my outrage certainly influenced my choice of words—or to make it fit other professions. Eventually someone posted a video on YouTube of me performing the poem live, and that's when it really took off. Millions of people have now watched and listened to the poem. It seems I was lucky enough to capture in words what many people have thought but never quite been able to say.

In two different ways, the poem "What Teachers Make" changed my life more than it did anyone else's. First, it changed my job. When I wrote the poem I was still teaching in a regular classroom. But two years after writing it, I decided to put my teaching career on hold—to "quit my day job," as they say—to see if I could pay the bills as a touring poet and advocate for teachers. I now make my living traveling around the world teaching poetry, talking to teachers about how to teach poetry, and simply reminding teachers why the path they have chosen to walk is noble, valuable, crucially important, and rewarding, despite the snide comments they may get about their paychecks. I'm following my dream.

But "What Teachers Make" changed my life in another, more appreciable way as well. People started to become teachers after reading it or hearing it. I started getting e-mails from college students telling me they had changed their majors to education and that I was at least partly responsible for their decision. That made me feel like I was making a difference in people's lives. So after a couple dozen people told me that they had decided to pursue a career in education after reading the poem, I gave myself a goal: I would convince one thousand people to become teachers through nothing more than the passion with which I spoke about the profession. I called it the Quest for One Thousand Teachers. Suddenly I had a new purpose in my life. I had a vision of something larger than myself. And on a practical level, I had another reason to write every morning. And that has had a profound impact on me. I am not just writing to delight and instruct anymore, I am trying to change the world, one teacher at a time.

Of course, in the grand scheme of things, even after I finally reach my goal of helping to create one thousand teachers, I will have done virtually nothing to help improve education in the United States. Serious inequalities remain in the way schools are funded, and teachers are under attack for being lazy and incompetent. These are problems that require more than poetry. In fact, sometimes I think I make the problems worse! What am I, really, but a propagandist who mollifies teachers into accepting the status quo? I sometimes feel that way when I am worn out from the fight. But I always come back to the fact that being a teacher is one of the greatest jobs in the world, and sometimes the people who have chosen to walk that noble path simply need to be reminded that there is a vast army of educated and grateful citizens who has their backs. Someone needs to remind teachers that they are dearly loved. I'm that guy.

The whole object of education is . . . to
develop the mind. The mind should be
a thing that works.

Sherwood Anderson (1876–1941),
American novelist and
short story writer

MAKING KIDS
WORK HARD

Whenever someone challenges me about what teachers make, my first answer is that teachers "make kids work harder than they ever thought they could." The most important thing a teacher can do is make students apply themselves. Some achieve it through gentle coaxing and encouragement while others use fear and intimidation. I would argue that both strategies are forms of love. Simply put, the best teachers are the ones you work your tail off for because in the end you just don't want them to think any less of you. You want and need their approval.

There's a story about President Nixon's secretary of state, Henry Kissinger, that I like to tell students. Kissinger asked an aide to produce a report. The aide submitted his report, but it was returned to him later that afternoon with a note from Kissinger that said: "I'm sorry. This is not good enough." The aide felt like he'd been busted because he knew Kissinger was right. So he sheepishly took it back and revised it. He made the report significantly better and re-submitted it, but it came back again with a similar note: "This is still not nearly good enough." Now the aide was scared! He canceled his plans for the eve-ning and stayed up all night working on the report. He caught careless errors he hadn't seen before and added a section of analysis that tied the whole thing together. He felt he had done his absolute best work, so instead of just submitting the report as he had done twice before, he made an appointment to de-liver the report to Kissinger personally. "Mr. Secre-tary," he said, "I have written this report three times and twice you have sent it back saying it was not good enough. Sir, what I am handing you now is the absolute best I can do, so if it is still not good enough, then I am not the right person for the job." Kissinger thanked him, smiled, and took the report, adding, "Excellent. This time I will actually read it."

It was this story I was thinking of when I wrote the line in "What Teachers Make" about how teachers can make an A– seem like "a slap in the face." When you do not submit your absolute best work for evaluation, everyone loses. So an A– really can be an insult to a student who is capable of A+ work.

But the other part of that line is just as important: "I can make a C+ feel like a Congressional Medal of Honor." An outstanding teacher knows that when a struggling student truly applies himself and earns a C+ on an assignment, it is entirely appropriate to write underneath the grade: "Congratulations!"

In the long run the ability to work harder than you ever thought you could may be the most important thing a teacher can teach. The actual subject matter is not the real lesson you want your students to learn; the real lesson is learning how to keep going even when what you're learning is hard and confusing. When the student inevitably asks, "When are we ever going to need this in real life?" the answer is not what they expect: *never.*

These exact facts, figures, and problems? You'll probably never need them. The real lesson here is the diligence, cooperation, resilience, flexibility, critical thinking, and problem solving you are actively using today. You will use those skills every time life presents you with something difficult or unexpected: obstacles in your personal life, accidents and catastrophes, lost jobs and loved ones. Working through those challenges is what matters most. When I'm teaching kids to work harder than they ever thought they could? That is what they will need every day of their lives.

Education is too important to be left solely to educators.

Francis Keppel (1916–1990),
U.S. Commissioner of Education
(1962–1965)

YOUR CHILD IS
MY STUDENT

reat teachers will never be able to make up
for bad parents, nor should they ever be
expected to. And yet it happens all the
time. Teachers are called upon to fulfill the role of
parents because they are the next most visible care-
givers in a child's life. When I was a sixth-grade
homeroom teacher who also taught math and history, there were some students of mine who I suspect
saw more of me than they did of their parents. It was

not uncommon for a student to pass by his mother or father briefly at breakfast and maybe again at dinner for a total of less than an hour every day. Compare that to the hours of face-to-face time I got to spend with children Monday through Friday and it's not hard to see how a teacher might appear to be a reasonable substitute for a parent. Except that we never are.

There is one thing that teachers can sometimes do that parents cannot: see a child's potential objectively, untainted by family history and parental expectations. A mother or father might be too preoccupied with how one child compares with another to be able to fully appreciate the uniqueness of the individual child. Or else parents use their children's lives as a redo of their own, ignoring the reality that such do-overs are unfair and unwise and usually impossible. It seems obvious that sending your daughter to an Ivy League school won't really make up for the fact that you might have been accepted to one if only you'd worked a little harder. Maybe your kid is lazy just like you were. More likely she's completely different.

So when you come to a parent/teacher conference and complain to me about your son's grades because "my son is an A student!" just be ready for my answer: "I suspect that is true. Now how can we get him to do A-level work this year?"

THE RACE CAR PROBLEM

Imagine there's a car competing in a 100-mile road race. Halfway through the race, the car makes a pit stop and the crew chief determines that its average speed so far is 50 mph. How much faster must the car go in the second half of the race in order to end up with an average speed of 100 mph for the entire race? I loved putting this question on math quizzes because the answer is surprising and enlightening. It's a trick question of sorts because the answer is that there's nothing the race car can do to double its average speed. It has already taken too much time in completing the first half of the race to hope to double its average in the second half. Even if it went 200 mph in the second half (the most tempting answer), it would complete the course in another 15 minutes. But the average speed would still come out to be only 80 mph. It's just too late. The car would have to instantly beam itself to the finish line 50 miles away at the speed of light in order to average 100 mph. Too much mediocrity has been allowed to pass for acceptable progress to make certain levels of excellence possible. The best the car can do is to revise its expectations for the outcome of this race and promise to do better in the next one. I think of this story often when a student or parent comes to me midway through the term to ask what can be done to salvage an A for the term.

> Like the old farmer from Maine giving directions, I have to tell them, "You can't get there from here."

I once had a student named Samuel in an eighth-grade English class. He had been diagnosed with ADHD and was taking medication for it, which he hated; he said it took away the part of him that felt familiar, the part that he recognized as being Samuel, and left in its place a stunned thirteen-year-old who couldn't do anything except follow directions. He was still struggling in my class, especially with our weekly vocabulary quizzes. I suspect his medication, which he took in the nurse's office every morning, had worn off by the time he finally got around to studying his vocabulary words in the afternoon or evening, and his brain was once again moving too fast to focus.

I had not been in favor of putting Samuel on

meds for his ADHD; instead, I wanted those of us who taught Samuel to use different methods to teach him, such as the one I discovered one afternoon on the soccer field.

Samuel was the goalie on the boys' middle-school soccer team, and occasionally I would stick around after school to scrimmage with them just to get a little exercise. Since I, too, had been a goaltender, the coach would sometimes send me off to work with Samuel one-on-one before or after the scrimmage. I remember one afternoon in particular because it was the day before one of our vocab quizzes, and Samuel needed to do well on it to keep a passing grade. The quizzes tested only ten words at a time, but there was no faking it; you got two points for spelling the word correctly, five points for writing out a complete definition, and three points for using the word in a sentence that demonstrated understanding. (In other words, "I'm feeling very *enervated* today" would get you nothing.)

Samuel's study habits were obviously not working, so after the game, as it began to get dark, we stayed on the field and while I drop-kicked soccer balls at him, I had him define the words on the next day's quiz. (I still remember two of the words because he kept mixing them up: *impolitic* and *myopic*.) He loved it! And it worked very well—not just with the words but with his goaltending. When he got a word wrong, I pretended to be outraged and kicked the ball even harder. Samuel would make a spectacular save and nail the definition the next time. He aced the quiz the next day.

Teachers have a unique perspective. We generally don't have to pick up dirty laundry off the floor of the bathroom or enforce bedtimes. Consequently we see our students through more dispassionate glasses than their parents do. We are more likely to notice the repercussions if a dancer is being pressured to become a mathematician or the writer of imaginative short stories is being pushed into science. By the time these students enter the workforce, many of the jobs they will apply for will be in industries that don't even exist yet. That's a hard future to prepare someone for. Teachers have their sights set on the real goal: not to produce Ivy League graduates, but to encourage the development of naturally curious, confident, flexible, and happy learners who are ready for whatever the future has in store.

The task of the poet is to delight or instruct, and we must reserve our greatest approbation for those who can do both at the same time.

Horace (65–8 BC), Roman poet

A POET BECOMES
A TEACHER
(AND VICE VERSA)

lthough I went to graduate school for poetry, I came out a teacher on the other side. Like all the graduate students in poetry, fiction, or rhetoric at Kansas State University, I taught Composition I and Composition II. Every college and university has some version of these classes; they're the ones everyone takes to make sure they didn't graduate from high school without knowing how to write passably. Personal reflections, evaluations, business letters, persuasive arguments, extemporaneous essays, and research papers: these were the types of writing we taught our students to produce. And I just had a knack for explaining how it is done.

That's what teaching is, the art of explanation: presenting the right information in the right order in a memorable way. The teacher's job is to sort through all those explanations and examples before class and to present the ones that work best . . . and then perhaps to leave off the last step so that the students can make that connection for themselves.

My uncle is the artist Vint Lawrence, and he told me that he asks three questions of a painting: (1) Does the artist have anything to say? (2) Does he or she say it well? And most important, (3) Am I allowed to finish the thought? The act of completing the thought for yourself is integral to the appreciation of a painting. A similar process is at work in the art of teaching; the best lessons are those in which students have been guided to the place where they can take the final steps themselves.

On weekends in grad school, when my fellow students and I gathered over beer and pizza, they all wanted to talk about the poems they were writing, but I wanted to talk about the papers I was grading. When we graduated, many of them went on to get PhDs so that they could teach older students, but I started substitute teaching because I wanted to teach younger students. I wanted to see if I could make more of an impact in students' lives if I got them into my class earlier, before they had learned bad habits. But the younger the students I taught—I eventually worked my way down to sixth grade— the more I realized that the most important work to be done in education is with the youngest possible kids, the ones in primary school and pre-primary.

From what I understand, the evidence is overwhelming: when children have access to quality pre-primary education, the advantage they get is so great that their peers who were not as fortunate will never catch up. Never. Even if I had been the greatest teacher in the history of the world, by the time a student reached my sixth-grade class, the extent to which he or she could progress intellectually had been almost entirely determined nearly ten years earlier! No wonder teachers will never be able to make up for the work that parents have failed to do.

I've never taught really young kids for more than a workshop or two, and although I've enjoyed every minute, I've always come away exhausted and filled with admiration and respect for their regular teachers. It's so different from what I'm used to! If I explain to the first grade that I once had a dog named Apollo (after the Greek god) and he died in November, it is then necessary to hear from every first-grader who has ever had a dog, a cat, or any other pet, has heard of Apollo, is Greek, or has a birthday in November. Then we have to talk about birthdays. For ten minutes. If I ever taught first grade regularly, I would teach a lesson called What I Wanted to Say but Waited Patiently Until Now to Say.

Managing the flow of curiosity is, of course, easier than policing other types of outbursts that occur with older kids. I found an old journal from when I first started teaching middle school that was filled with my day-to-day observations. On one page I had written this: "Being in middle school is all about making calculated attacks look like accidents and vice versa." I have seen boys put on their backpacks with wildly exaggerated swings designed to "accidentally" smack a neighbor in the chest with the full weight of a book bag. These are the same boys who, in a different situation, will take a dramatic dive on purpose, like an Italian soccer player looking for a penalty call against his opponent. The only strategy I ever developed for dealing with this behavior was simply to call attention to it, saying, essentially, "I know what you're doing, and you don't need to. You have my full attention. What can I do for you?" Because that's all many of us need—a little more attention from someone in authority.

People sometimes say that experiencing my work as a poet made them wish they'd had me as a teacher. Or else they say, "I can tell you were an excellent teacher." It's a great compliment, but it always makes me wonder whether I was a better teacher than I am a poet. What I do know is that since leaving the classroom, I've never stopped teaching. Everything I do is a kind of lesson, even if I am the only person who learns it.

CALLING
HOME

When I was teaching full-time, I used to stay at school late most Tuesday evenings just to make calls home to talk with parents. The school had a big Rolodex in the teachers' lounge, and we were encouraged to make calls on the school's dime. I was thinking of those calls when I half jokingly wrote the line in "What Teachers Make" that says, "I make parents tremble in fear when I call home." Really, who doesn't fear the worst when their child's teacher calls home? In fact, the first thing out of most mothers' mouths—and it was usually the mothers I spoke with—was "What did he do this time?" or "I apologize for whatever my daughter said."

Because they expect bad news, parents are invariably thrilled when teachers call home for *good* reasons. And I made more of those kinds of calls than the bad kind. A lot more.

I remember calling home to praise an improved quiz grade or compliment the obvious hard work that had gone into a revision. Sometimes I called just to say that I appreciated a simple comment made during class discussion that struck me as particularly astute or mature. Parents should be hungry for every bit of information you can spare. And if they are not, if they are never home, never return your phone calls, or are otherwise unresponsive or unconcerned about their children's progress in your class? Well, that, too, is good to know.

I quickly discovered three important lessons about making good phone calls to parents. First of all, those calls are easier and more fun to make;

there is no threat of the parent turning against you: "Well, what did you say to my daughter to make her call you stupid in the first place?! *Did you do something stupid?*" Second, there is no lingering doubt that you will actually be making things much worse for the child. Sometimes you can tell in just a matter of seconds exactly from whom Junior inherited his crazy, inconsistent, self-destructive behavior, and you know the call will have some repercussions you didn't expect . . . or want.

But the most important lesson to be learned about calling parents at home to praise the achievements of their children *is that those calls are actually more effective.* The student comes into class the next day with a lighter step, a brighter smile, and usually more of the same wonderfulness that prompted me to call home the night before. I once had a student named Caleb, a squirrely seventh-grader who rarely pushed himself very hard. I taught Caleb math, and one day he got a question wrong on a geometry quiz. I had written the question myself, and I recognize now that it was badly worded. But

Caleb wanted to argue the point with me in class. I was too smart to get into an argument with a seventh-grader during class time, so instead I challenged him to prove me wrong for homework.

That evening I called Caleb's mother. It was not the first time one of his teachers had ever called home—I got the sense that she was used to fielding such calls—but it was the first time anyone had ever told her anything good. I wanted her to know that the intellectual curiosity and vivacity that her son had displayed in class reminded me why I chose to teach in the first place. I told her that I loved my job because of kids like Caleb. The quality of silence on the other end of the phone told me that she was *crying*. By reaching out to her that night I had created an ally, someone I could call again in a month when Caleb was driving me crazy. "I wanted to strangle your son today!" I could joke with her, and she would laugh and joke back, "I can do it while he's sleeping and make it look like an accident."

There is one other story to tell about calling home, and it is the one that figures specifically in

"What Teachers Make"—about one boy defending another against the class bully.

Andrew Marks was in my sixth-grade homeroom and was bright, kind, rosy-cheeked, well dressed, and a little chubby. During recess one day, Andrew got involved in a card game of Uno with three other boys: Timmy, the littlest urchin in the grade; Travis, the meanest kid it has ever been my displeasure to teach; and a fourth boy whose name I don't remember whom I shall call the Bystander Who Did Nothing.

I don't know the rules of Uno, but apparently there are a couple of different ways you can play, various alternative rules and strategies that everyone must agree on at the beginning of the game in the same way poker players agree which cards are wild before the hand is dealt. The boys must not have confirmed in advance what the rules would be because early on in the game Timmy managed to successfully execute a very rare move, and the three others made him take it back. From what I could gather sitting at my desk grading quizzes, Timmy's play was roughly tantamount to "shooting the moon" in Hearts, a feat requiring equal measures of luck, cunning, and boldness. He was quite pleased with himself for pulling it off and was naturally crushed when the three other boys all told him the move was not allowed in that particular game, that they were "not playing that way." Timmy took his cards back, but his bottom lip began to quiver. Seeing that vulnerability, cruel Travis began circling for the kill.

"What? Are you about to cry!? It's just a game! And you're going to cry?! Look at Timmy, everyone, he's crying! What a big baby!"

I knew I needed to step in despite the fact that my intervention could make things even worse. But before I could stand up I heard Andrew confront Travis, saying, "Leave him alone. So what if he's crying? I still cry sometimes, don't you?"

And that was it. In the poem I call it the "noblest act of courage I have ever seen," and it still makes me shiver. Andrew was not exactly immune to Travis's cruelty; Travis could easily have started in on Andrew being fat for his size, as he often did.

Nevertheless, Andrew Marks, knowing that what he was witnessing was bullying, pure and simple, put himself between the bully and the victim and took the bullet. When I called his mother that night to tell her what had happened, I think I cried myself. I told Mrs. Marks that Andrew was the kind of student who made me proud to be a teacher and that I wanted to be just like him when I grew up. But I think my tears came from another place as well. They came from the shame of knowing that had I been a twelve-year-old boy in that card game, I would have been the Bystander Who Did Nothing.

LIGHTBULB
MOMENTS
AND HAPPY
ACCIDENTS

I f one could somehow graph the way a child learns, the line would almost surely *not* be a slow and steady climb toward knowledge and intelligence. Rather it would look like the jagged, volatile climb of the stock market in a good decade. Here the highest peaks would be those sudden moments of insight and clarity brought on by divine coincidences and other happy accidents, and the deep plunges back into adolescent lethargy would be the result of habit, hormones, and fear of greatness. Teachers often call the moment when something clicks in the mind of a student and he or she finally "gets it" a Lightbulb Moment. Witnessing them can be so exhilarating that they become some of the most rewarding moments of any teacher's career. It's part of how a teacher is paid—in the rare and beautiful bright sparks of cognition in the eyes of a struggling student.

One particularly memorable Lightbulb Moment for me occurred when I was trying to teach a student named Paul the Zero Product Property, which states that if any factor in a product is zero, the result will always be zero. Once you understand the Zero Product Property, it's hard to imagine ever having trouble with it, but such is the nature of the "curse of knowledge."* I remember crouching at the side of

---

* A Stanford graduate student named Elizabeth Newton studied the "curse of knowledge" in 1990 by having people tap out the

Paul's desk and softly explaining the property again. Suddenly his eyes got big, and he turned to me. "Are you saying," he began, as though not quite willing to believe his good fortune, "that five multiplied by three-sevenths, multiplied by 125, 342.8, multiplied by zero will be . . . zero?" When I nodded, he returned to his work excitedly, announcing to whoever was listening, "This changes everything!" And that is, in essence, what all teachers want to do: change everything.

---

rhythm of well-known songs such as "Happy Birthday" and "Jingle Bells" to other people who were then asked to identify the song. The "tappers" predicted that the "listeners" would be able to guess the song 50 percent of the time. In reality, the listeners were correct only 3 percent of the time.

I TEACH FOR THE FIRE

I teach for the fire, the moment of ignition, the spark,
the lightbulb of cognition going on in the dark
over an adolescent's head. O beautiful incandescence,
dazzling the dead air all around the room; he tries
and he tries and he tries and BOOM, he gets it
and you can see it in his eyes! I teach for that moment.

I teach for the moment all the elephants realize
they have wings and fly up out of the gutter,
my room aflutter with a thousand hummingbirds—
hovering in place, rapt expression on every face,
feeding on my words for one wild minute
like ideas were wildflowers. I teach for that moment.

I teach for the same reason every teacher teaches.
The pebble never knows how far the ripple's reach is,
but I restart my heart each day and learn things

> *about myself like I were an empty bucket and every*
>   *student*
> *a wishing well. They say those who seek to teach*
> *must never cease to learn. I teach for the moment*
> *everything catches fire and finally starts to burn.*
>
>   —*Taylor Mali*

Sometimes a Lightbulb Moment can be brought on by something totally unexpected, such as the time my students witnessed—or thought they witnessed—a change in the English language that usually takes years.

When I taught English, I used a vocabulary book that was divided into thirty chapters, each of which introduced ten new words all related to the same specific theme, such as Words Borrowed from Spanish or Words for Describing People. The first chapter was called "On Language" and included the words *connotation, denotation, jargon, slang,* and a word that was new to me, *argot,* which is the word for a kind of secret language used by a certain group, such as thieves, to conceal true meaning. I decided to come up with a homework assignment based on the argot of eighth-graders. "This language we speak belongs to you," I told them. "You might as well take advantage of it and create some secret slang of our own."

Each student was to invent ten expressions for school-related phenomena. As an example, I suggested that getting a detention might be called "shanking a D," as in "For passing notes in class, the teacher shanked me a D."* My students all nodded their heads and eagerly began doing their homework out loud, suggesting, for example, that the secret eighth-grade slang expression for getting an extension might be *to hang yourself from a higher branch,* whereas requesting permission to visit the

---

* I much prefer what one student came up with for receiving a detention: *booking a one-way ticket to statue class.*

bathroom when you don't really have to go might be secretly referred to as *puddling* or *begging a false flush*. The bell rang and half the class left, the other half remaining for their section of American history taught by my colleague Mr. Robert Crust.

Bob Crust was a forty-year veteran teacher, and his eyesight was poor. Nevertheless, he spotted one of my worksheets on a desk where it must have been forgotten by one of my more careless students only minutes before. Bob gave the assignment a cursory reading and concluded—almost correctly—that *shanking a D* was already established slang among hip middle-school students. So at the end of his class, in explaining the consequences for anyone who came to class unprepared on Monday, Mr. Crust casually announced that "any such shirkers can definitely expect to shank a D." Half the class was utterly mystified as to what he meant.

But the other half? The students who had seen me for English the period before were incredulous! How could Mr. Crust know that expression already when they had only learned it themselves an hour ago? When it hadn't even existed before that?! Could the English language be alive!? Just like Mr. Mali said it was!? The absolute highest goals and objectives of my lesson, goals and objectives I didn't really have any right to expect my students to achieve—an understanding of how language changes over time and how meaning can be fluid—were attained in the instant that small group of students looked at one another in wide-eyed amazement. What do teachers make? They make use of happy accidents to drive their lessons home.

The object of teaching a child is to enable him to get along without a teacher.

Elbert Hubbard (1856–1915),
American author, editor, and printer

DEFINITELY
BEAUTIFUL

Funnily enough, when I perform "What Teachers Make" in front of large groups of people, especially but not necessarily teachers, I invariably see heads nodding in understanding when I get to the line about making students write the words *definitely* and *beautiful* over and over again "until they will never misspell either one of those words again." Sometimes I even add the word *business* to create my personal trifecta of misspellings: definitely beautiful business.

I learned how to spell the word *definitely* in ninth grade from my English teacher, Stewart Moss, who sang for the entire class "The Definitely Song," a mnemonic device that he claimed would keep us from misspelling the word forever. It has a high, sweetly melodic tune, and it goes like this:

> *There is no A*
> *in definitely.*

That's the whole song. The entire freshman class stared at Mr. Moss and said, "That's it?! That's the song that's supposed to teach us to spell the word *definitely* correctly for the rest of our lives? That's not going to work! I'm going to forget that before I go to sleep tonight!" But that was in the fall of 1978 and I still remember it perfectly.

Beautiful doesn't have a song that goes with it, but it sticks in my head because of a particular Lightbulb Moment. The summer after ninth grade I went to a summer school because my parents felt I had sloppy study habits, which I did. In my humanities class I sat next to a wrestler named Larry. One day Larry asked the teacher how to spell the word *beautiful*, adding that he had never been quite sure. The teacher told him to look it up but warned him that it would probably take him the remaining twenty minutes just to find the right dictionary page. She was right. And when Larry finally found the word, he kept repeating the first four letters out loud incredulously as we packed up our things and headed to lunch, "B-E-A-U?! That's how it starts?! B-E-A-U?! I never would have guessed!" He said it so many times that some of us began to parody the four-letter litany of his astonishment. But deep inside I was actually grateful. Larry wasn't the only person who had never been entirely sure of how to spell *beautiful*. But now we're both sure to remember.

Needless to say, I have sung "The Definitely Song" in classrooms full of students hundreds of times. Sometimes I even sing it through twice, adding extravagant musical flourishes while channeling my inner lounge singer, but I have no evidence to suggest that my need for more stage time has improved the power of the original. What's more, every time I have told the story of how I learned to spell *beautiful*, it ends with my own students listing off the first four letters in their own dramatic and deliberate renditions of Larry-the-wrestler's grateful wonder.

But there is a larger point about these two backstories that I really wish I had managed to work into the poem somehow: the exhilaration that comes with all epiphanies, those unforgettable bursts of new understanding. We tend to think of learning in the same way that we imagine a child grows taller: as a gradual, steady process marked by occasional spurts of accelerated progress. But the process of learning is more like a series of minor and major lightning bolts that strike the brain constantly. And if you have ever witnessed one of these moments occurring in someone else, then you know why teachers say it's one of the secret joys of the profession. Especially if they helped make it happen. Teachers make lightning strike over and over again.

KEEPING YOUR EYE OUT FOR THE TEACHABLE MOMENT

A t times when you are a teacher life presents you with a much better lesson plan than the one you prepared, and you just have to go with it. You won't have any time to figure out what kind of homework to assign to draw out the lessons from that moment . . . you just have to wing it.

Once when I was teaching a math class at a school in New York City, something extraordinary happened outside the window. My classroom was on the fourth floor, but because the ceilings of the school were quite high, we essentially looked directly into the sixth-floor apartments in the building across the street, which was only about fifty feet away. This provided more than enough distraction on a near daily basis. There was the young woman who leaned out the window to smoke and actually kept her cigarettes hidden on the corner of the ledge that was just out of view of anyone inside the apartment. There was an old guy a floor above her who shuffled around his apartment all day in his bathrobe. If he saw you he would wave, so we called him Mr. Happy, and I grew to hate him because he was an irresistible distraction for my students. But even Mr. Happy was no match for the grand piano that was pushed out a window on the floor above him.

I found out years later from a friend who lived in that same building that there was a woman on the eighth floor whose dream it was to give a piano recital at Carnegie Hall. She must have talked about it so much that her wealthy husband finally decided to rent out the hall so she could fulfill her dream. Apparently, however, the pianos at Carnegie Hall were not good enough for her. No, she insisted that if she were going to play Carnegie Hall, it would have to be on her own piano. This was why, on a random Thursday in April, a flatbed truck with a crane pulled up in front of the building, and her grand piano was expertly pushed out her window and lowered slowly past my classroom window as I tried to teach math.

By the time the piano was entirely out the window, all of the chairs in my classroom were empty. We pressed our faces to the window and fogged the glass with our fascinated breath. No one said anything. Was there any way I could relate this to the math lesson? Maybe "How many fractions do you think the piano will break into if it drops?" I could think of nothing. But that was okay because there was nothing to say. It was a visually stunning and epically memorable moment, and I remember wishing only that I could command such attention as a teacher. As the piano was lowered slowly past our

window, I saw out of the corner of my eye Mr.
Happy in his bathrobe, staring at the piano between
us. He waved, but for once everyone was mesmerized by something else, and no one waved back.

UNDIVIDED ATTENTION

A grand piano wrapped in quilted pads by movers,
tied up with canvas straps—like classical music's
birthday gift to the criminally insane—
is gently nudged without its legs
out an eighth-floor window on 62nd Street.

It dangles in April air from the neck of the movers'
*   crane,*
Chopin-shiny black lacquer squares
and dirty white crisscross patterns hanging like the
*   second-to-last*
note of a concerto played on the edge of the seat,

the edge of tears, the edge of eight stories up going
    over—
it's a piano being pushed out of a window
and lowered down onto a flatbed truck!—
and
I'm trying to teach math in the building across
    the street.

Who can teach when there are such lessons to be
    learned?
All the greatest common factors are delivered by
long-necked cranes and flatbed trucks
or come through everything, even air.
Like snow.

See, snow falls for the first time every year, and
    every year
my students rush to the window
as if snow were more interesting than math,
which, of course, it is.

So please.

Let me teach like a Steinway,
spinning slowly in April air,
so almost-falling, so hinderingly
dangling from the neck of the movers' crane.
So on the edge of losing everything.
Let me teach like the first snow, falling.

—Taylor Mali

[Education is] . . . going forward from cocksure ignorance to thoughtful uncertainty.

Kenneth G. Johnson (1922–2002),
American educator and semanticist

IN PRAISE OF
THOUGHTFUL
UNCERTAINTY

One of the most important qualities that a teacher can encourage in a student, especially in the age of the Internet and cable "news" shows, is the ability to sift through information and distinguish between what is useful, objective, and reliable, and what is biased, tangential, and ultimately forgettable. Consider the British historian George Macaulay Trevelyan, who once wrote: "Education . . . has produced a vast population able to read but unable to distinguish what is worth reading."

I always wanted my students to leave my classroom with a kind of educated skepticism, the ability to question the reliability of their sources for faulty logic or bias instead of learning things by rote or taking them on faith. This desire is what lies behind the line in "What Teachers Make," "I make them criticize." The verb *criticize* has two definitions, of course, one neutral (*to assess or analyze the merits of*) and the other overwhelmingly negative (*to disparage, condemn or carp*); people have asked me over the years if I meant that I was trying to turn my students into obsessive nitpickers. I wasn't. But nitpicking when it comes to facts is not such a bad thing, is it?

To encourage my students to argue against positions that don't hold up under scrutiny, I put essay questions on tests that required each student to respond to an "excerpt from a scholarly work." The quotation was always one I had made up myself; it was entirely fake, as was the title of the essay or book from which it purportedly had been excerpted.

But I did my best to make them sound convincing! Who would dare pick an argument with Dr. Sanjay Patel, the learned scholar and author of *Sphinx in the Sand: Religion in Ancient Egypt*? Well, after reading his asinine conclusion that "religion in ancient Egypt was not an important part of society, and as a result priests were relatively powerless," my students would be raring to politely but systematically rip Dr. Patel's ideas to shreds!

Rarely will you find a description of a teacher as someone who shows students how to *Question Authority* (in the words of the famous bumper sticker). In fact, many critics of American education have argued that schools do exactly the opposite because the system we have in place now grew out of the early industrial revolution's need to create compliant, adequately skilled but ultimately obedient workers. How could thoughtful skepticism, to say nothing of pure and simple creativity, survive such an environment? Not easily. But I'd rather teach my students to be people who know how to doubt rather than people who sound as if they never had any doubts at all.

TOTALLY LIKE WHATEVER, YOU KNOW?

In case you hadn't noticed,

it has somehow become uncool

to sound like you know what you're talking about?

Or believe strongly in what you're saying?

Invisible question marks and parenthetical (you know?)'s

have been attaching themselves to the ends of our sentences?

Even when those sentences aren't, like, questions? You know?

Declarative sentences—so-called

because they used to, like, DECLARE things to be true, okay,

as opposed to other things are, like, totally, you know, not—

have been infected by a totally hip

and tragically cool interrogative tone? You know?

Like, don't think I'm uncool just because I've noticed
    this;
this is just like the word on the street, you know?
It's like what I've heard?
I have nothing personally invested in my own
    opinions, okay?
I'm just inviting you to join me in my uncertainty?

What has happened to our conviction?
Where are the limbs out on which we once walked?
Have they been, like, chopped down
with the rest of the rain forest?
Or do we have, like, nothing to say?
Has society become so, like, totally . . .
I mean absolutely . . . You know?
That we've just gotten to the point where it's just,
    like . . .
whatever!

And so actually our disarticulation . . . ness
is just a clever sort of . . . thing

to disguise the fact that we've become
the most aggressively inarticulate generation
to come along since . . .
you know, a long, long time ago!

I entreat you, I implore you, I exhort you,
I challenge you: To speak with conviction.
To say what you believe in a manner that bespeaks
the determination with which you believe it.
Because contrary to the wisdom of the bumper sticker,
it is not enough these days to simply QUESTION
    AUTHORITY.
You have to speak with it, too.

—Taylor Mali

True education makes for inequality; the inequality of individuality, the inequality of success, the glorious inequality of talent, of genius.

Felix E. Schelling (1858–1945), American educator

ENCOUNTERING GENIUS

I am well aware of what it's like to come face-to-face with someone half your age with twice your brainpower. The single most intelligent student it has ever been my pleasure to pretend I was teaching was named Ellen Perlman.

In the early 1990s, fresh out of graduate school, I lived for a while in southern Maine and became the associate editor of a small literary magazine. To pay the bills, I was a substitute teacher and a tutor for The Princeton Review, a company that helps students learn to improve their scores on standardized tests such as the SAT, GRE, and LSAT. After doing these three jobs for a year, I went looking for a permanent teaching position and ended up at Cape Cod Academy, a school desperately looking to replace a teacher who had to move away midyear. That teacher had taught English, advised the school's literary magazine, and coached all the sophomores and juniors on how to take the SAT. Everyone was a little baffled at how perfectly the job fit me; they made jokes about how the position was tailor-made for Taylor Mali.

After I had been on the job less than two weeks, a massive earthquake in the Japanese city of Kobe indirectly resulted in two students joining one of my SAT preparation classes. One of them, a winsome junior named Sarah, had actually been in Kobe on a study abroad program, but the earthquake had so damaged the infrastructure of the city that it made more sense for her to come home and finish out her junior year at her old school. She joined my class to prepare for the SAT because it was required of all juniors. All juniors, that is, except for one.

Ellen Perlman, Sarah's best friend, didn't have to take my class because she was a genius, and everyone knew it. She had taken the SAT at the beginning of her junior year (before I arrived) and received a perfect score, so she certainly didn't need my prep class. Nevertheless, when Sarah returned to school after the earthquake, Ellen started coming to my SAT prep class just to be with Sarah instead of spending the time in the school library reading *The New Yorker* and *Paris Match*. For weeks, she never said a thing, and I wondered why everyone thought she was so smart. Then one day while I was struggling to explain how to solve a math problem, Ellen raised her hand and offered a suggestion.

I wish I could remember the exact nature of the problem I was trying to explain to the rest of the class. It was tricky, involving geometry and at least a couple of variables. I had done my best to draw the figure on the board and was in the midst of muddling my way through my explanation when Ellen said something like this:

Mr. Mali, perhaps it would be helpful if you considered the problem this way. Reflect the rectangle you have drawn along the axis AB so that you end up with a square. Now imagine that square is the base of a pyramid that projects into the room and meets at a point let's call X some distance from the blackboard. The distance between X and point C is clearly the square root of the sum of the squares of AB and BX, isn't it?

I was absolutely gobsmacked. Her logic was ingenious, intuitive, and disarmingly brilliant. I think I may even have gotten down on my knees and flailed my arms in her direction, chanting, "I am not worthy!" And here's the thing: her answer made sense! When you could finally wrap your head around it, it was perfectly clear! Considering the problem from her point of view—her singularly beautiful, creative, and dazzlingly luminous point of view—was definitely "helpful." Even more, it was definitely beautiful.

There have been many other instances in my teaching career when I have come to understand in a single lightning bolt of awareness that I was dealing with someone whose brain just worked better than mine did. Someone mentally nimbler, more shrewd, with greater cognitive dexterity. Just plain smarter than me. And that's fine. In fact, it's a blessing. A humbling blessing. Teachers shouldn't make the mistake of always thinking they're the smartest person in the room.

You teach best what you most need to learn.

Richard Bach (1936–),
American author

THE STUDENT
BECOMES
THE TEACHER

F or a week a few years ago I was the visiting writer-in-residence at The American School of London, a beautiful cathedral to learning just a few minutes' walk from Abbey Road and the famous studio where The Beatles recorded their album of the same name. The student body of ASL is typical of international schools the world over, a worldly rainbow of the children of diplomats and businesspeople. The particular students with whom I worked—the entire eighth grade, as I remember—

were eager to learn the different types of poems that I had planned to teach them how to write. But what I taught the students that week is not what I suspect most of them will remember about the week I spent with them.

For the first three days of my residency—a Monday, Tuesday, and Wednesday—I had each section of the eighth grade for two forty-five-minute classes a day. That gave us plenty of time to go over the poems they had written for homework, to discuss the new type of poem we would be working on, to read a few famous examples, and to answer questions. And of course there was time to write in class as well. I could even give the students mini assignments that I expected them to complete by the time I saw them later in the day! Then we could talk about their work, and I could modify what I wanted them to do for homework. I couldn't have asked for a better schedule for teaching poetry! I taught "how to" poems, five-senses poems, inanimate-object poems, sonnets, haikus, "I remember" poems based on Joe Brainard's famous book-length poem of the same title, and many others. But one assignment worked better than all the others, and we devoted all of Thursday to it. On that day, my eighth-grade students taught the third grade how to write their favorite type of poem.

I'd arranged for the third-grade teachers to bring their classes to the library. We had already paired each eighth-grader with one or two of the third-graders. So during the opening minutes of class, the groups got to meet each other while I explained what we would be doing. And then it was off to a quiet corner to write a poem together, one "big" kid of twelve or thirteen, and one or two "little" kids of eight or nine. I knew that good work was being done when there was absolutely *nothing* for me to do. I visited each group and eavesdropped, listening to how my students chose to explain the concepts they had only just learned themselves a few days before. I took lots of pictures, and all the while I smiled like a fool.

When I had the idea for this project, I don't know whether I knew about the research that suggests the best way to really learn something is to turn around and immediately teach it to someone else. I certainly hadn't heard of groups like The Breakthrough Collaborative, a summer school for underserved but highly motivated middle-school kids that is taught by high school and college students. All I knew was that it worked. The act of teaching something to someone else sticks it in your brain better than anything else; knowing that they would be teaching on Thursday made my eighth-graders pay particularly close attention earlier in the week.

At the end of the period, we gathered in the comfiest corner of the library and had our own little poetry reading. Children from all over the world—the Middle East, Western Europe, Asia, Australia, Africa, and elsewhere—sat and listened to one another's poems, occasionally coached by their eighth-grade mentors. I sat with the third-grade teachers and the two librarians, my stupid smile interrupted every so often by quiet tears.

You cannot teach a man anything;
you can only help him find it within
himself.

Galileo Galilei (1564–1642),
Italian physicist and astronomer

MY BEST DAY AS
A TEACHER

The best moment of my teaching career—
and there have been many good ones—
occurred in Kansas in the early nineties and
involved one of those Lightbulb Moments I wrote
about earlier. I tell the story in greater detail in another poem of mine called "Like Lilly Like Wilson,"
but here's essentially what happened. (I changed the
identifying details a tiny bit in the poem itself.)

In Manhattan, Kansas, in the early 1990s I was a
ponytailed liberal from New York City who drove a

black Ford Mustang convertible, possibly the most idiotic car for weathering Kansas winters but wonderful for speeding through the rolling prairie hills of northeastern Kansas in the fall and spring. So when the student I call Lilly Wilson first told me she wanted to write a persuasive essay that argued in favor of making it illegal for gay couples to adopt children, I said nothing, afraid that if I tried to dissuade her I would look like what everyone else already assumed I was—a long-haired, hippieish, liberal, Marxist weirdo—and she would only become more entrenched in her opinion. All I did was remind her of the requirements of the paper, the number of different sources she needed to have, and the questions to ask of those sources to make sure they were reliable. She came to me after only a few days of research and asked if she could switch sides because the evidence she had discovered did not support what she thought it would. In "Like Lilly Like Wilson," I write that I wanted to tell Lilly, "You make me feel like a teacher, and who could ask to feel any more than that?" But there is another series of lines that even more accurately describes what was going on for me in that moment and why I consider that day the best of my teaching career:

And I want to tell her . . .
[that] changing your mind is one of the best ways
of finding out whether or not you still have one.
Or even that minds are like parachutes,
that it doesn't matter what you pack
them with so long as they open
at the right time.

Those are two truisms I probably read on bumper stickers growing up, but what greater lesson is there to teach anyone than how to have an open mind? There is no better outcome of one's education, which the American philosopher William Durant called "a progressive discovery of our ignorance." That's one of two definitions of education that I think of when I think of "Like Lilly Like Wilson." The other definition is, of course, George Bernard Shaw's: "a succession of eye-openers each involving the repudiation of some previously held belief."

The takeaway lesson for me was that I will never be able to teach anything to anyone as well as they will be able to teach it to themselves if given the opportunity. So maybe that's what the definition of teacher should be: someone who makes learning possible, which often means simply preparing the ground for you to teach yourself.

E-MAIL, ISLAM, AND ENLIGHTENMENT (INSHA'ALLAH)

One of the best single projects I ever taught was unofficially called the Muslim Internet Buddy Project. I was teaching seventh-grade medieval history in New York City, and one of the chapters in the textbook was on the founding and rapid spread of Islam. This was in the late nineties, so the world had yet to be turned upside down by 9/11, but even then I recognized in my students the year before a truly unpleasant attitude toward Muslims. The first year I taught that chapter on Islam, my students made a lot of ignorant jokes about taxi drivers, which made sense in New York City, since virtually the only Muslims any of them ever saw drove taxis. But it was wrong, and I knew it, even if I never was able to make some of them see why. So the next year I vowed to do a better job teaching that chapter.

I came up with a plan and asked a couple of people for help. The only Muslim family at the school that I knew of was a Turkish family who had a sixth-grader in my ancient history class. He wasn't part of this project because he was a year too young, but his mother helped me nevertheless, giving me the names and e-mail addresses of several of their friends back in Turkey, including children about the same age as the ones I was teaching. A Muslim friend of mine from graduate school did the same with members of her family in Pakistan and several of her friends who were still in graduate schools all across the United States. In the end, I was able to pair each student in Medieval History with an e-mail correspondent who was a follower of Islam, a Muslim Internet Buddy.

Not every student had a personal e-mail account the way they probably would today, so the school's technical director created special e-mail accounts for all my students, accounts they could only access from school. For a few days, we spent a portion of each class coming up with what we thought were good and appropriate questions, such as, "What's it like to fast for the entire month of Ramadan?" and "Which of the Five Pillars of Faith do you find most difficult to follow?" Then we spent a class in the computer lab and everyone wrote to their buddy, introducing themselves and asking their questions. I asked them to CC me on all their e-mails and to instruct their buddies to do the same.

We waited a few days before we went back to the computer room, during which time we covered more of the chapter and devised new and more informed questions. Finally the day came when we got to see if we had received any replies. And we did! In fact, most of them did. There were a few no-shows—life does tend to get in the way—so a couple of kids needed to share the buddies who seemed more responsive. But oh, the noise and excitement in the room! Everyone wanted me to read how their buddy had answered their questions! They were reading messages from people born on the other side of the world (never mind that some of them were studying at Columbia University less than two miles away).

What we discovered—and this was a surprise to me as well—was that most of the Muslim Buddies didn't actually consider themselves particularly good Muslims. Some did not fast at all during Ramadan, others couldn't even name all of the Five Pillars of Faith! They considered themselves Muslim, sure, but it wasn't the most important thing about who they were. This was the starting point of several great class discussions about faith and identity. We discovered that not a single member of the class, myself included, could name all of the Ten Commandments from memory.

Want to know what most of the Muslim Internet

Buddies wanted to talk about? Michael Jordan and the Chicago Bulls, who were tearing up the NBA during those years. Basketball, American TV, and pop culture. Some of my students found this comforting and dove into the project with renewed enthusiasm. The wiser students found it curious and perhaps a little sad. But everyone's eyes were opened, and no one made any jokes about taxi drivers that year or ever again while I taught at that school. In fact, on more than one Monday morning, I heard stories about conversations my students had started with delighted New York City cabdrivers.

What we have to learn to do, we learn by doing.

Aristotle (384–322 BC), Greek philosopher

LESSONS YOU
CAN TOUCH

'm a big fan of projects that require you to build or draw something to demonstrate your understanding of a topic. Mixing things up, creativity in the service of learning—it's all part of being an effective teacher. My old nemesis from the National Poetry Slam, Daniel Ferri, also a teacher and poet, has a poem called "Backwards Day" in which he recounts refreshingly different approaches to learning various lessons:

In math class, for homework
Describe the associative, distributive, and commutative
*   properties*
In dance
Choreograph it, dance it, show your work
Points off for clumsiness

In Social Studies, for homework
Prepare two Civil War marching songs, one North one
*   South*
Sing in four part harmony, show your emotion
Points off for flat notes

In English, for homework
Carve a sculpture that expresses Hester Prynne's solitary
*   courage*
The cowardice of her lover
The beauty and strangeness of her child

In Science, for homework
Bring in a broken toaster, doorknob, or wind-up toy
Fix it
You get extra credit, for using the leftover parts to make
*   something new*
Points off for reading the directions

No matter what the subject or age of the students, teachers would be wise to tap into children's natural desire and ability to build, create, innovate, and express. I decided to experiment with this one year by creating the Greek Shield Project for my ancient history class.

The assignment was simple: make a shield informed by your knowledge of the shield designs of such Greek city-states as Athens and Sparta. But there was a twist. This was not to be some namby-pamby shield made out of poster board that I could use to decorate the walls of my classroom; this shield needed to protect you. Protect you from attack . . . with a sword. And everyone knew what sword. The year before, I had taken my medieval history class on a field trip to Medieval Times, a chain of arenas that stage nightly jousting tournaments while mesmerized children wearing paper crowns feast on turkey legs and quaff soda from plastic goblets. At the end of the night, before getting back on the bus, I purchased a full-size metal replica of an Excalibur-like sword such as might have been used by the

Knights of the Round Table. I kept it locked in a cabinet in my classroom, and it became known as *The Sword of the Realm*, a name always proclaimed with a kind of chivalric gusto, and answered—I don't know who started this—by the entire class chanting the reverential incantation "Oooh-ha-ha!"

I told the boys—it was an all-boys school, but I would have assigned the same project to a coed class—that on the day the shields were due, I would attack each of them with the sword, and if the sword pierced the shield and caused injury or death, then they would get a bad grade, too. They loved the prospect of danger, even though, in reality, all the attacking would happen to the shield stand the school's custodian built for me out of two-by-fours with quick-release clamps on the sides.

There was, of course, an artistic element to the Greek Shield Project. In fact, 30 percent of the grade was based solely on how colorful and imaginative the design on the outside of the shield was. We were familiar with some of the traditional designs used in ancient times, and my students knew exactly how much they could stray from those designs in terms of color. Another 30 percent of the grade was reserved for what we called *structural ingenuity*—the way each student chose to solve the problem of attaching the shield to his arm. Did it involve a leather strap and a screen-door handle screwed onto the back of the shield? Or was it a single handle in the middle of the shield made from a metal trash can lid inverted so that the convex outside was now the concave inside?

But the most important part of the assignment—the remaining 40 percent of the grade—was based on the shield's effectiveness, or, as we called it, its *defensive integrity*. When each boy's shield was clamped into the slingshot-shaped shield stand, how well would it withstand two direct blows from *The Sword of the Realm* (Oooh-ha-ha!)? The first strike was a broadsided blow we called the Smack Test, the second, a skewering lunge we called the Poke Test. We would all find out on the day the shields were due, a day that came to be known as Smack Day!

Smack Day was in early April, and I wish I had

taken pictures of the boys with their shields as they milled about on the sidewalk before school—not so much for the gloriously incongruous vision of neatly dressed private school boys all packing colorful ancient Greek shields, but for the look of unadulterated pride and joy on the faces of my students. The expressions of students not in my class, as well as those on the faces of innocent passersby, ran the gamut from envy to quizzical alarm.

How each shield held up under attack from the sword depended almost exclusively on the choice of material for its construction. Several students built their shields starting with a circular plastic sledding disc. They were no match for *The Sword of the Realm* (Oooh-ha-ha!). The Smack Test would usually crack the plastic, and then the sword would slip through the crack on the Poke Test. Shields made out of metal trash can lids survived the Smack Test, providing a dramatic and satisfying clang, but were easily skewered by the sharp metal blade during the Poke Test. Surprisingly, the shields made out of various types of wood fared the best. Then again, that makes perfect sense because wood is the exact material the ancient Greeks used to construct their shields! You have to see it in action to understand why it works.

Smack Day was a huge success, my only wish being that the school's insurance policy had allowed each student to attack his own shield. And of course I did end up hanging some of the most colorful and dramatically battered shields on the walls of my classroom, where they served as living reminders of history at work, Smack Day, and *The Sword of the Realm* (Oooh-ha-ha!).

Education is an admirable thing, but it is well to remember from time to time that nothing that is worth knowing can be taught.

Oscar Wilde (1854–1900),
Irish poet and dramatist

THE VALUE OF WHAT YOU CANNOT TEST

or all of our scientific achievements and medical discoveries, the human brain and how it works are still largely mysteries to us, and that eventually affects educational policy and how we teach our children.

As any business consultant will tell you—I actually have a good friend who said this word for word—"If you can't measure something, then you don't know what it is." Well, guess what? Curiosity, imagination, the process of education, the complex ways people learn, even how the human brain actually works—no one really knows how to quantify them, or just what makes them tick.

No wonder the path of least resistance is to stick blindly to the state-approved "script" in every subject, the one that prepares students for the tests that measure their comprehension of those scripts.

"Who cares if the students' eyes glaze over?" a beleaguered teacher might ask. "In less than a year they won't be my problem anymore, and I might still have a job."

There's a Buddhist saying: *Trying too hard to achieve one objective will achieve its opposite.* Anyone who has been forced to "teach to the test" only to see their students' scores continue to decline has firsthand proof that the Buddhists nailed it.

In the summer of 2011 I recited "What Teachers Make" at a rally for teachers in Washington, D.C., called the Save Our Schools march. It was a scorching hot Saturday in July, and I got to share the stage with some educational visionaries such as Diane Ravitch and Jonathan Kozol. But the speaker most of the thousands of gathered teachers were waiting to hear was actor Matt Damon, who in recent years has become a real champion of teachers and an advocate for public education. After being introduced by his mother, Nancy Carlsson-Paige, a professor of early childhood education, Damon said this about the connection between his public school education and who he has become:

> *As I look at my life today and the things that I value most about myself—my imagination, my love of acting, my passion for writing, my love of learning, my curiosity—all of these things came from the way that I was parented and taught. And none of these qualities that I prize so deeply, that have brought me so much joy, that have made me so successful professionally—none of these qualities that make me who I am can be tested.*

If teachers were allowed the freedom to teach the best way they know how, they could design lesson plans and activities that would encourage in their students a passionate pursuit of knowledge or even just simple curiosity. They might discover, as I have, that your progress in all of your cognitive pursuits will be greater if you work on them all simultaneously rather than focusing on one at a time. In other words, learning a foreign language is easier if you are also memorizing mathematical concepts, working with watercolors, learning to play a new instrument, trying to grow a tree from the pit of an avocado, and learning to ride a unicycle. I don't know why. I just know. And teachers do, too. What do they make? Teachers make use of their knowledge (when they are free to do so).

Perhaps the most valuable result of all education is the ability to make yourself do the thing you have to do, when it ought to be done, whether you like it or not.

Walter Bagehot (1826–1877),
British economist, essayist, and critic

NO ONE LEAVES
MY CLASS EARLY
FOR ANY REASON

I n my first year of teaching middle school I learned that when class gets a little tedious or tense (perhaps I get irritated by punchy, pre-lunch behavior), students start trying to leave to get a drink of water or go to the bathroom. We do the same thing as adults in meetings or at parties. Sometimes we just don't want to be there, so we look for any opportunity to just break up the routine.* Who hasn't made up an excuse to get out of an awkward or boring situation? Still, my students needed to figure out that much of life is simply learning to buckle down and do what you have to do even though you don't really feel like doing it. So I instituted a policy that no one was ever allowed to leave my classroom for any reason. Ever. Especially not to get a drink of water. I made a few concessions for girls when I taught at a coed school, but when I taught all boys, my students were mine for the entire class period, from bell to bell.

I wasn't trying to be mean or teach a hard lesson about life. Great teaching moments happen in the

---

* I left the classroom before cell phones became as widespread as they are today, so I never had to deal with texting in class. A school nurse shared with me one of her favorite diabolical strategies for dealing with this issue: whenever she finds herself in possession of a confiscated cell phone, she texts all of that student's friends from the phone with the following message: "OMG! Make up an excuse to get out of class and meet me in the nurse's office ASAP!" Then she waits in her office with a stack of detention slips to hand out to whoever shows up.

classroom all the time when you least expect them! It would be a shame if a student missed one just because he or she had a short attention span or had a habit of cutting out when things got slightly uncomfortable. Very quickly, my students just stopped asking to leave my class. They stayed for the entire period no matter what was going on in class, and they tuned in even if they didn't want to. And that's all I wanted—and was trying to teach them—in the first place.

I have never let my schooling interfere
with my education.

Mark Twain (1835–1910),
American writer

MY BAD
(APOLOGIZE
AND MEAN IT!)

How to apologize when you are wrong is not likely to appear on any state's educational curriculum, but learning how to say you are sorry is a skill and an art, and an absolute necessity. It was definitely part of the core curriculum in my classes.

My students and I practiced apologizing and discussed the nuances of offense, humor, sensitivity, and contrition. Some may disagree, but I believe that a sentence that begins with the phrase "I owe you an apology" is not actually an apology itself. If you owed someone money, you would not consider your debt repaid by simply acknowledging it. You need to follow through. You need to actually say the words *I am sorry* by themselves, without any qualifications before or after. This means that you can't even say, "I apologize if my remarks offended anyone." That's a politician's apology, not a real one. And don't try the old "I was just joking" excuse, either. If you were joking, then everyone should be laughing. Tacking "I'm just joking!" or "Just kidding!" at the end of an insult does not automatically make it a joke.

I had one sixth-grader, Ryan, who was vivacious and intelligent but had a real temper that was, for the most part, under his control. Imagine a stick of dynamite with a short but soggy fuse: hard to light, but dangerous if it ever catches. Some of the other boys in his class occasionally made a game out of seeing how close they could get to making Ryan explode. And when he did, it was all fists and elbows, and people got hurt. The victim in these outbursts was usually a kid named Bart, but to be fair, Bart was also the worst antagonist. When I got Ryan and Bart together after one of their battles, Bart would sit and sob convincing fake tears while explaining disingenuously how he had tried to take the high road and hadn't done anything wrong. There were apologies needed on both sides, of course, but the ones Bart gave TO Ryan were the most useful, and the most honest: "I'm sorry that I find it so entertaining to provoke you. I promise to stop." The apology shifted the conversation from consequence to cause, and everyone walked away with a better sense of the work they needed to do in their own hearts. It was a lesson that didn't appear on any test . . . but one that all of us could probably use a refresher course on every now and then, myself included.

MEG: MALI'S ELECTRONIC GRADE BOOK

'm a moderately computer savvy guy as long as you're talking about Apple computers. I got my first Mac in 1985, and I've never owned anything else. So when I started teaching, I used ClarisWorks spreadsheets to keep track of quizzes, tests, essays, and everything else that went into calculating my students' grades. I became a man obsessed with formulas and cells and the type of number crunching that would have kept me up late at night but which a computer can do without thinking. Still, when I met with students to discuss their progress in my class, I had to perform a kind of semaphore dance with blank pieces of paper to keep them from seeing their classmates' grades. Either that or I would print and then cut out long ribbons of numbers and hand the paper snakes to my students. It was a math teacher who told me that a spreadsheet application was actually not what I should be using. "What you want is a database."

In my last four years teaching in a regular classroom, I discovered the database application called FileMaker, and I used it to design an electronic grade book that revolutionized not just my record keeping but how I interacted with students concerning their progress. A database is just like a spreadsheet except there is no need to look at all of your information all of the time. You can customize certain layouts that contain only what you need. Different kinds of information can easily be obtained by clicking on different layouts. I designed my grade book around my own needs, of course, but since I wanted it to be useful to other teachers as well, I started with a few basic premises that I thought would apply to most teachers.

I assumed that most teachers would want to determine each student's final grade using a weighted average of separate scores, with a little "wiggle room" for things like class participation, attendance, lateness, and behavior. Some of the scores might be averages themselves, for instance, a homework average, a quiz average, a test average, an essay average, and a project average. Teachers could tweak the program to account for more of some kinds of assignments and fewer of others, and then decide how much each average would count toward the overall grade. My new electronic grade book was adopted by several teachers at the school, and it changed my relationship to grading in several significant ways.

First of all, it allowed me to easily keep track of a student's progress as the term progressed instead of waiting until the week before grades were due and staying up late several nights in a row crunching numbers and realizing some students had never turned in certain assignments. I could keep on top of everything from the outset because it was now easy and fun. I frequently invited students to look at the layout of their grades for the term. We could run different scenarios to see how well they would have to do on the chapter test and the final essay if they wanted to "salvage a B+." As a result, there were never any surprises at the end of the term; my students knew exactly what grade they were going to get, sometimes to within a fraction of a single point.

Depending on the subject and the type of assignment, grading can be a subjective art. As a teacher, you need to be able to explain why one assignment is unacceptable, another is average, and a third is above average or even exemplary. And I could certainly do that, either in my comments or in a one-on-one conference. But when it came time to put it all together, I found it comforting to have the computer's mathematical wizardry behind me to avoid long whining sessions with grade-grubbers. It's hard to argue with an overall average of 86.142857. That's a B. Congratulations. Next.

The electronic grade book also made a difference with regard to the narrative comments all teachers had to write for each student at the end of the term (narrative comments were given along with the overall grade and an effort grade). Most teachers started with an obvious boilerplate paragraph about what the class had studied during the term and then wrote a separate paragraph specifically commenting on that student's progress and achievement. Not me. Using the various merge functions available through the database, my entire report was personalized for each student. Both parents and administration wondered how I was able to produce so much analysis so fast.

The truth is that the program was doing a lot of the laborious work of spotting patterns for me. All I had to do was tell it what patterns to look for and what kinds of comments to return whenever it identified them. For instance, a high quiz average and a low test average usually means the student suffers from test anxiety or is being thrown by the essay section of the tests. But the opposite (low quiz scores and high test scores) indicates a smart but lazy kid who blows off the homework and crams for the tests. I spent hours and hours writing code that would identify patterns and spit out what I called "skeletal comments," which I would then analyze and personalize further because obviously not every kid with an overall average of 72 deserves the same comment; it depends on where he or she has come from at the midterm. Trending progress was the key factor. Thus the basic language of the skeletal comment that the computer program suggested as appropriate was largely contingent upon two things: whether the student's final average was higher or lower than it was at the midterm, and whether that difference was substantial or remarkable, significant or appreciable, or hardly noticeable at all.

In this particular instance, technology made me a better teacher. I loved using it, and it made me more responsive to my students' progress and better able to identify the areas in which they needed improvement. Make no mistake, it was not the testing and the grading that made me a better teacher; it was how I was able to respond to the results to craft more effective strategies for each student. Teachers, if they are lucky, make use of technology that helps them become better.

TRUNCATING VS. ROUNDING

My grading program actually got me rethinking the entire concept of "rounding." Rounding numbers, I realized, is a sloppy human invention, an exigency to make calculations easier. But computers don't need to make calculations easier. Why, then, do I still need to do it? I realized I didn't. If an A- starts at 90, and your average is an 89.5, well, that isn't 90, is it? At the end of the term, when each student has amassed several months' worth of grades, it becomes very difficult to nudge your overall term average up or down unless a specific assignment—a test or an exam—counts for a significant percentage of the overall grade. And you expect an unearned "gift" of an entire half point simply because twenty-five years ago most teachers would have done so just to make their work simpler? I don't think so.

The inventor of the system deserves to
be ranked among the best contributors
to learning and science, if not the greatest benefactors of mankind.

Josiah F. Bumstead (1797–1859),
on the invention of the
chalkboard

TEACHERS MAKE
TECHNOLOGY
WORK!

I am a big proponent of old-fashioned memorization, perhaps one of its last known fans. I know
from memorizing new lines of poetry that the
memory is a muscle, and the more you use it, the
stronger it gets. So in every class I taught, no matter
the subject, there was always a fair amount of simple memorization that was required, whether it was
the square of every number up to twenty, the factors that contributed to the fall of the Roman Em-
pire, or just a simple poem to recite in front of the

class. All my classes contained mini-lessons in mnemonics, a system to develop or improve the memory, and in many, my students had to create their own flash cards.

I noticed while building and tweaking MEG (Mali's Electronic Grade Book) in FileMaker that a file could be specified as either a single- or multi-user document. This meant several people could modify it at the same time . . . for instance, all my students. I became very excited; I just needed the right project. Would I use it in my history classes? Or in my math class? I decided to use FileMaker to help my ancient history students develop an infinitely expandable *communal* deck of flash cards they could then use to study for the next test.

For homework a couple of nights before a chapter test in Ancient History, I asked my students to come up with fifteen review questions of their own and to bring them to class along with the answers. Meanwhile, I was working on the layout of the electronic deck: there was a button for creating new cards, and another for rating the difficulty level of each question. Finally, there was a button that said NEXT that would automatically switch to the question-only layout and go to the next card. I took a couple of screen shots of the deck and showed them to the students the next day so they would be familiar with the look of it.

Finally the day came to visit the computer lab and create flash cards. Everyone brought their questions and answers with them, and when I told my students they could begin typing in their review questions, the room filled with the beautiful silence of good work being done. Dave Stevenson (the school's director of information technology) looked at me and we smiled. "That is the sound of success," he whispered. No one had any questions about what they were supposed to do, and as a result no one was tempted to bother anyone else. Every student had a manageable task to do and was eager to start completing it. Pretty soon the students noticed that the deck of flash cards was growing at a rate well over ten times faster than the speed at which they were working individually. After typing in only a few questions each, the total number of cards in the deck was well over thirty! They began reading one another's questions and revising their own questions to make them better.

By the end of the class, everyone was simply clicking through the deck, tweaking and editing the questions and seeing how many of the answers they knew. They were also rating the difficulty of each card, and this led to several discussions about what made a good question good. Before they left, I showed the class a final layout that listed all the best questions and their answers, which by that time numbered around two hundred, in a small but readable font on one or two sheets of paper. Not a deck of flash cards, but a list of all the questions and their answers. Everyone got to take a copy home to study with.

In retrospect, the project was a success for a couple of important reasons. First, we used the technology effectively because we did a lot of work first and knew what we were going to do with it. Second, because everyone was working together on the same deck of flash cards, there was a collective aspect to the project that was driven by pure generosity. Students took pride in their questions and complimented one another on well-worded ones that tested their knowledge. It also gave the students a safe and anonymous way to gauge their familiarity with the material a day before the test; those who encountered several review questions that stumped them realized they would need to put in a little extra time studying. And lastly, it must be pointed out how important it was that our school could afford a computer lab where no one had to share a computer. Although that is as it should be, it is rare, even in a private school. Those kids were lucky.

The past does not repeat itself, but it rhymes.

Mark Twain (1835–1910),
American writer

THINKING IT THROUGH: THE TIMELINE AT THE BACK OF THE CLASSROOM

🍎

Middle school is a fascinating time in a child's development because it's when the brain starts becoming more comfortable with greater degrees of abstraction. When I taught eighth-grade English, I could—and often did—ask my students to write one or two paragraphs that *might conceivably* appear in the middle of a hypothetical five-paragraph essay. But when I tried that a couple of years later with a sixth-grade history class, the students kept asking when the whole essay would be due. They couldn't comprehend the idea of writing a body paragraph of an essay they would never actually have to complete. That vantage point—a front-row seat inside a child's thought process—often yields insights that help you improve your teaching . . . and students' thinking.

When I taught ancient history, the first chapter in the textbook covered our earliest human ancestors—the various species of the *Homo* genus that culminated in us, Cro-Magnons, as well as our anthropological cousins the Neanderthals. Every chapter after that was devoted to a different ancient civilization in a very rough chronological order, beginning with ancient Sumeria and continuing with the civilizations of Egypt, China, Africa, and the Americas. It was fascinating stuff, and my students loved it as much as I did. But I discovered something about how the middle-school mind keeps track of time: every single student believed that all of ancient Chinese history happened long after everything in ancient Egyptian history. The events couldn't have happened at the same time in history because we studied China in February and Egypt way back in October! Never mind that the dates in both chapters were contemporaneous—in a kind of meta-temporal way, the students thought that whatever they learned about first must have happened first.

When I discovered this, I created a twelve-foot-long timeline on the bulletin board at the back of my classroom that stretched from 3100 BCE on the left (the approximate year King Narmer unified the Upper and Lower Kingdoms of Egypt) all the way to 410 CE on the right (the sack of Rome by the Visigoths). I painstakingly measured out 350 decades in centimeters, labeled them clearly, and then sealed the whole thing under clear packing tape. And that's how the year began: with a blank stretch of just over 3,500 years during which, apparently, nothing happened.

As we began to study each new ancient civilization in the textbook, I created little sticky notes for the major events and accomplishments, briefly noting the event along with the year it occurred. I used Post-its that were about the size of a stick of gum and I cut one end into a point to more accurately place them on the timeline. At the end of every class, I had about half a dozen events to stick on the timeline, and it became a highly coveted honor to be chosen for the task. And since the events were written on sticky notes, after one class left, I could pluck them from the timeline so that another section of the same class could repeat the task for themselves. At the end of the day I taped all the new events permanently in place with another layer of clear packing tape.

But here's the thing: I've never been one of those teachers who is obsessed with dates. Sure, you need to know a few when the test rolls around, but what I really wanted was for my students to know that history was happening all the time, all over the world simultaneously, as it always had been. The real learning occurred not when a student stuck an event in the right place on the timeline, but when he or she noticed what other events were already there from the chapter or two before. The effects of a massive volcanic eruption? The spread of iron weapons and alphabets? I remember one student considering a thousand-year span and asking me with wide eyes, "Could the Ten Commandments have been influenced by Hammurabi's Code?!" It was one of the best questions I'd ever been asked, and of course there is only one answer. "What do you think?"

We make a living by what we get, but we forge a life by what we give.

Winston Churchill, (1874–1965),
British prime minister

WHAT TEACHERS GET: PRESENTS FROM PARENTS

🍎

No one becomes a teacher to get rich. Anyone who chooses to enter this profession does so for other reasons, most of which are priceless (either because no amount of money can purchase them or because they are utterly without monetary value). Hilarious misspellings, thank-you notes years later, confessions of tipsy parents at holiday parties, and the laughter of children: these are some of the lucrative benefits that are never mentioned in anyone's contract. And, of course, there are the holiday presents.

Holiday gifts are not universal. Some schools actually prohibit parents from giving them at all. And some teachers won't accept them to avoid the appearance of impropriety. Or else they accept only home-baked goods. And of course some parents can't afford presents for their own children, much less for their teachers. But then there are the inexplicable gifts that you love, like the bottle of Western Musk cologne that one student gave me. It was the most foul-smelling concoction ever, and I kept it in my desk and used it as a particular type of punishment. If anyone was unprepared for class, he got a full squirt of Western Musk right in the chest. The smell became synonymous with unpreparedness, even with my students from years before. "Uh-oh," I would hear them say in the hallway when they caught a whiff of it, "someone was unprepared."

But the best holiday gift I ever received as a teacher was indirectly related to a gift certificate for dinner for two at the Four Seasons, a fancy restaurant in New York City. It was from the parents of a sixth-grader named Liam, who was struggling in class. I didn't see a conflict of interests; the parents and I both knew that whether Liam passed or failed my class would be entirely up to Liam himself. Besides, my wife was a chef at the time, and we were slowly working our way through the best restaurants in New York City and calling it research.

So one Friday night in mid-December we treated ourselves to an extraordinary meal—the seven-course tasting menu complete with wine pairings—and that night I dashed off a quick thank-you note to Liam's parents. I don't remember everything I said in the note, but I do remember joking that I had briefly considered ordering a $1,800 bottle of wine but decided not to press my luck with their generosity. I ended the note expressing my hope that Liam would do better in my class the next term. About a month later, I found a note in my mailbox in the teachers' lounge saying that there was a package waiting for me in the front office.

If you think Liam's parents sent me the $1,800

bottle of wine, then you're like most people, because that's what everyone expects when I tell this story. That would make at least a kind of ostentatious sense and would have made a good yarn. But that's not what happened. Instead, what was waiting for me in the front office was an exquisitely wrapped package about the size of a framed diploma with a note from Liam's mother. "Dear Mr. Mali," it read. "Thank you so much for your wonderful thank-you note! We loved it so much we have had it framed and are giving it back to you. Happy New Year!" Sure enough, inside the package was my own thank-you note professionally framed with a complementarily colored matte border and covered in UV-coated protective museum-quality glass.

What did this mean!? Were they somehow insulted by my note? Were they really hoping that a fancy dinner would buy their son a passing grade in my class? More to the point: WHO IN THEIR RIGHT MIND FRAMES A THANK-YOU NOTE?! Maybe if it was from the president or the Pope, but even so, if they loved it enough to frame it, why would they give it back to me?! It suddenly became clear to me that Liam's parents were nuts. Or they thought I was.

Unfortunately, Liam's performance in my class—and every other—took a turn for the worse and he didn't return to school the following fall. I truly regret not being able to help him. And almost as much, I regret not saving the framed thank-you note, or at least inserting it into a shadow box with the accompanying card and sending it back to Liam's parents.

FIGHTING BACK AGAINST THE ATTACK ON TEACHERS

Teachers are under attack, and I'm not surprised.

We live in a country of unchecked greed and excess, where everything and everyone has been slowly squeezed bloodless so as to maximize earnings for a tiny fraction of the population. Profit in the short term has come to trump sustainable and equitable long-term growth, to say nothing of environmental preservation. Any proposal that even mentions the words *fairness, responsibility,* or *common good* is labeled "socialist" and dismissed outright. Government, one of whose very purposes is to accomplish collectively through laws what individual citizens cannot do for themselves, lacking either the means, authority, or willpower (even if it is in their best interest), has been crippled by accusations of "overreaching." In an environment like this, why should anyone be surprised that the voracious machine has finally set its sights on teachers?

The only thing that surprises me is the characterization of teachers as lazy and greedy. Only someone with very little understanding of what teaching requires would say such a thing. Certainly teachers themselves can do a better job of letting the world know how hard their profession is, but frankly, they have real work to do and a lot of it, so they don't have a whole lot of free time on their hands. Whenever I hear someone on television talk about how easy teachers have it, I want to put them in their own classroom for a year to see how they survive. Of course, that wouldn't be fair to the students. An idiot might learn his lesson, and it might make for captivating reality TV, but it would come at the cost of a classroom full of students who deserve better. And that's just not worth it. Then again, there are thousands of classrooms across the country that already deserve better than what they are getting.

Here's a fact I never hear anyone on television talk about: all the teachers I have known need at least one hour outside the classroom for every hour they spend in the classroom. So the next time you hear someone talk about the paltry number of hours teachers put in every day, double it. That may sound like a lot, but teachers need this time for meeting, planning, and preparation beforehand, and evaluation, grading, and counseling afterward. So even if you assume that teachers get to school at eight in the morning (few teachers I know get to school that late) and leave at three in the afternoon (again, I've *never* met a teacher who was able to leave that early), that is still a fourteen-hour workday if you account for the hours necessary to support those hours spent in school. Not every hour spent in school is spent in class. True. But if you factor in time spent in administrative and departmental meetings, supervising other school activities, and commuting to and from school, there is very little time left in the day to eat meals, spend time with your family, not to mention sleep. It's not a sustainable workweek.

Two things happen to teachers as a result of not having enough time in the day to prepare for their classes. The first is that they need to outsource most of their planning and preparation time to the summer so that during the school year they can concentrate on evaluation, grading, and counseling. My great-aunt taught for forty years, and I remember during summer vacations watching her prepare letters and numbers for the bulletin boards in her classroom. Years later, when I was a middle-school teacher myself, I spent a solid month going over my assignment sheets from the previous year, fine-tuning the scheduling of tests, quizzes, and other assignments. *When do I need to assign the first essay next fall so I can return the first drafts to my students in time for their revisions to be turned in before the October break so I can grade them and be able to base their mid-term narrative reports on something other than their quiz, test, and homework averages?* That's just one of the dozens of questions teachers might ask themselves over the summer about every one of their five classes. And God help them if they don't have all that stuff planned out before school begins.

There's another thing that happens when teachers realize that seven hours of working in school requires an additional seven hours of work out of school prepping and grading: teachers burn out. They quit. Fifty percent of all teachers in the United States quit by the fifth year of teaching. It's just too much work for too little pay. Compare that to the 3 percent teacher turnover rate in countries such as Finland and South Korea, whose students consistently score the highest on international achievement tests such as the PISA (Program for International Student Assessment), which is administered by the

Paris-based Organisation for Economic Co-operation and Development.[*] Teachers' salaries are injurious to the profession. And to add insult to injury, teachers are being called greedy!

Describing teachers as greedy makes as much sense as describing profiteering as altruistic. It's wrong and just plain mean-spirited. Teachers spend well over one billion dollars of their own money every year on vital classroom supplies that school budgets can no longer cover.[†] How is that greedy? Teachers get their summers off, but unless they're married to someone with a better-paying job, most have to work during the summer to make ends meet. In fact, it is not uncommon for teachers to have second jobs *during the school year* just to survive financially.[‡] In what universe could that possibly be called greedy?!

---

[*] McKinsey & Company's 2010 study "Closing the talent gap: Attracting and retaining top third graduates to a career in teaching."
[†] 2010 National School Supply and Equipment Association study.
[‡] Watch the 2011 movie *American Teacher* to see an example of how this can destroy a marriage.

I remember one payday about a year before I left the classroom. After lamenting once again that the amount didn't even contain a comma, I detached the check from the voucher of the same size that always came with it in the envelope from the business office. I had already put the check in my wallet and was about to rip up the voucher when one of my students, Stephen Parsons, walked into my classroom. "Hi, Mr. Mali. Oh, is that your paycheck?" Stephen asked. Instead of answering him, I ripped up the voucher before his eyes. Of course, there was no way for Stephen to know that it was only the voucher I had destroyed because the paper is the same. Stephen was convinced I had just ripped up my check, even though I had not answered his question. To carry the ruse a little further, I looked him dead in the eye and said, "I don't do this for the money, Stephen. I do this because I love it. And besides, the paltry sum I'm paid could hardly be called money anyway." Despite my best efforts to assure Stephen I was joking, rumors quickly spread that I was an independently wealthy heir of an old New York family who didn't need to work for a living but nevertheless chose to teach simply for the love of it.

The truth is that teachers *don't* teach for the money. The people who enter this profession these days do so because they want to make a difference working with children. What do teachers make? We make sacrifices. Daily. We do what we can to make ends meet. We're educated professionals who are passionate about what we do. We're not tough guys like truck drivers or sanitation workers; perhaps that's why we get pushed around more and paid less than truck drivers and sanitation workers. Teachers don't generally go on strike, and when we do, piles of garbage don't start accumulating immediately next to the mountains of undelivered goods. Sometimes I wish they would because then people would demand an immediate change.

WHERE DO THE BEST TEACHERS END UP?

Everyone needs a good teacher, and the best teachers should go where they are needed most. Unfortunately, that's not the way the system works right now. As long as we continue to tie the funding of public schools to local property taxes, the highest-paying teaching jobs will always be at schools in the wealthiest neighborhoods, and they will be filled by the most experienced teachers. Meanwhile, the school districts in neighborhoods with essentially no property tax basis will be left to hire new teachers with no experience who will almost surely try to move on after a year, either to another district or, too often, to another profession.

We need to make it easier for people to see if teaching is for them, if they are natural teachers. I have met hundreds of people who would have made outstanding teachers—who possess that rare, charismatic ability to make children focus on a specific task—but who will never get the chance to teach because life got in the way; they had a family to raise and never got a chance to finish their degree. Most states have some kind of non-college-campus-based route to alternative certification, and the total number of teachers certified through these programs each year has been on the rise until recently. We should do what's necessary to restart that trend.

Let's start a national conversation about the best qualities for teachers to possess and whether these qualities can be taught. The best way to train teachers is to put them in classrooms and watch them teach. Universities that delay student-teaching until the end of the degree program have it backward!

Put the baby in the water to see if it can swim; if it looks like it has a natural ability, then teach it how to swim even better. But if the baby looks like it's going to drown, pull it out, dry it off, and encourage it to major in something else.

WHY ATTACK TEACHERS AT ALL?

Without a gentle contempt for education no man's education is complete.

G. K. CHESTERTON (1874–1936),
BRITISH AUTHOR

Teachers will always be the object of criticism. I understand and accept that. At the very least, this criticism will be the kind of "gentle contempt" that G. K. Chesterton said was actually required of an educated person. It's inevitable. Why? Because the goals of education make it an easy target. They are so noble and lofty, so irreproachably optimistic—to

> *improve the minds of children so they may have a brighter future—that in reality, almost all efforts will fall miserably short. The disparity between what education is supposed to do and what actually gets done is so great that it is ripe for ridicule. It is human to secretly enjoy watching the fall of the high-and-mighty idealists. And since teachers, in theory at least, have the highest and mightiest and most idealistic calling of them all, they often bear the brunt of the ridicule when reality sets in. It comes with the territory, or in this case, the classroom.*

Certainly the education system in the United States is filled with teachers who are no longer effective. Every profession has its slackers. But for some reason, the national conversation about education always seems to revolve around the worst teachers in the system. Probably because it's entertaining to laugh at the lazy and incompetent, or the clueless teacher who points absentmindedly to things on the blackboard with his middle finger and then wonders why the entire class is giggling uncontrollably. I get it. The problem is that the critics of education love to hold up these folks and pretend that they are representative of teachers everywhere—that they prove the entire system is irreparably flawed and should be scrapped altogether.

What we need is a radically new organizing principle whereby the teachers who can teach effectively in the poorest districts have a financial incentive to go there. And that does not just mean the veteran teachers with years of experience; thirty years of teaching math in the suburbs doesn't necessarily mean you can last one year in the inner city. It takes a certain kind of skill set to be an effective teacher in the most demanding conditions. But an individual with those skills needs to be richly rewarded for bringing them into the communities that need them most. And that might mean that a relatively new teacher ends up earning more in the inner city than a teacher with more experience teaching in the suburbs. I have no problem with that. But many people do.

THE IMPORTANCE
OF MENTORING

For a little over a year after grad school, I was a substitute teacher in and around Portland, Maine. As anyone who has been a substitute teacher can tell you, it's miserable. Since the regular teacher can't really count on your having any knowledge in his or her subject area, you are usually reduced to proctoring quizzes or pushing play on the classroom VCR or DVD player. And since you don't know anyone's name, it's hard to keep any kind of order. People who call teachers "glorified babysitters" are thinking about substitute teachers (or should be). Still, for all its tedium and frustration, substitute teaching does give you valuable experience in classroom management. Everyone should do it for a while.

But even with college courses and some substitute teaching experience under my belt, I was still nervous when I prepared to take on my first "real" teaching job at a school on Cape Cod. I was teaching eighth- and eleventh-grade English and a special SAT preparation class for sophomores and juniors. But the school didn't throw me into the classroom unsupported. Once a week I met with Rick Bellamy, head of the humanities department, who had been teaching for almost twenty years. Rick and I would go over my plans for the coming week. To this day, I think I learned more about teaching and lesson planning in those forty-five minutes every week than I ever did in any college education class.

In teaching, if you don't have a finely developed sense of timing, either you end up panicking when the bell rings because you have covered only a fraction of what you needed to teach that day, or you may burn through your entire lesson plan in no time and find yourself staring at children with nothing to do—which, depending on the students, can be dangerous. Rick Bellamy would look at a simple activity I was planning to complete in the first ten minutes of class and tell me that it would probably take twice as long as I anticipated. With other activities Rick would say, "They'll be done with this in five minutes. Then what will you do?" I remember working just as hard to prepare for that one weekly meeting with Rick as I did for my classes.

I got lucky. New teachers should always have a mentor like Rick. Imagine if it were common practice to reduce the course load of a few veteran teachers in every school so they could mentor new teachers? Perhaps for the last five years of a veteran teacher's career, he or she could transition into more of a full-time mentor role, observing new teachers' classes often. I can't think of a more graceful way for a teacher to transition into retirement while at the same time taking advantage of his or her decades of experience.

The practice of classroom observation is so valuable that it would be hard to find a school that doesn't claim it is an important part of how they support and evaluate their faculty. Unfortunately, as most new teachers will tell you, few schools actually live up to the standards they set for themselves when it comes to observing teachers. If there don't seem to be book-burnings or prizefights happening daily in a new teacher's class, it's not uncommon for a new teacher to be observed only once in the first year and then not again for a couple of years or more.

A few times in my teaching career, everything fell into place perfectly and I had exactly enough time to complete what I had planned for the period. I returned and reviewed the previous night's homework, transitioned into the new material, explained how it all fit together and how it would be tested at the end of the unit, previewed the homework that was due the next day, answered questions, and finally, with one eye on the sweeping second hand of the classroom clock, said, "Well then, class . . . is . . . dismissed," just as the bell rang. Sure, I got lucky. But luck favors the well prepared, and mentors like Rick Bellamy made sure I was.

I am not a teacher: only a fellow-traveller of whom you asked the way. I pointed ahead—ahead of myself as well as of you.

George Bernard Shaw (1856–1950),
British dramatist, critic, and writer

TEACHERS
WHO MADE
A DIFFERENCE
FOR ME

I f having even just one truly exceptional teacher in your life makes you lucky—and I think it does—then my life has been an absurd embarrassment of riches. In a world where many people claim never to have had a single teacher who made a difference for them, I find it difficult to remember any teachers I had who were even mediocre, much less downright bad. It's possible that I was particularly ignorant and very teachable, but I know for a fact that I was—and still am—bizarrely lucky.* I can remember the names of most of the teachers I've had, from my first-grade teacher—Mrs. Keithline—to all my professors in graduate school, and many of them were outstanding. But I want to single out three.

Kate Millonzi was my fourth-grade teacher at the Collegiate School for Boys in New York City. That was her first year at the school, but I think she had taught for a few years at another school before coming to Collegiate. Kate read out loud to the class at least once a day, all of us sitting at her feet in ever-widening concentric semicircles. I remember a story she read to us about the Buddha and how he was thirty years old before he ever witnessed human suffering. She put the book down for a moment and looked up and said, "He was my age before he ever witnessed suffering. Imagine that." Unfortunately,

---

* Starting with my father, my first teacher, whose greatest gift to me was the love, respect, and devotion he had for my mother, which I grew up witnessing daily, year in and year out, until the day he died.

none of us found that as interesting as the fact that she had inadvertently told us how old she was. "You're thirty!?" Kate Millonzi made a difference for me because she loved me, and I would do anything to avoid the look of disappointment that occluded her face when I didn't do well. If that meant working harder and behaving better, so be it. Mrs. Millonzi, you made a difference in my life.

Jerome Dees was a Renaissance scholar and the head of the graduate studies department at Kansas State University, which meant he was familiar with all of us, even the poets and the fiction writers he would not otherwise have taught much in his own classes. Looking like a cross between Albus Dumbledore and Floyd Pepper, the guitarist in *The Muppet Show* band, Jerry Dees could be seen relentlessly jogging around campus almost every afternoon. No doubt the running was how he stayed so energetic despite his age, which was rumored to be upward of 150. In many meetings, some involving hoppy imported ales, Jerry helped me learn to love expository writing. Under his guidance, I developed a style of ultra-clear, hyperorganized writing that has served me well, perhaps even in my poetry as well. Jerry always respected the intellect of his students. I'll never forget the time he started to ask a class a question and then stopped. "Never mind," he said. "I know the answer to my own question, which really makes it more of a quiz, doesn't it?" He didn't want to insult us by asking a question to which he already knew the answer. To me, that made a difference.

But the greatest single teacher I ever had was Joseph D'Angelo, my fifth- and sixth-grade English and homeroom teacher at Collegiate. Dr. D, as we called him, had a PhD in semiotics, communication, and culture, and—even more impressive to us at the time—he was a black belt in Okinawan karate. And he sang opera! The man was smart enough to make you learn, big enough to force you to learn, and cultured enough to sing about the whole experience! I learned most of what I know about basic expository writing during the two years I had him as a teacher. And fifteen years later, when I was teaching freshman composition classes, I heard myself repeating his maxims—"Tell them what you're going to tell them, then go ahead and tell 'em, then tell 'em what you told 'em"—to my college freshmen! I've stayed in touch with Joe over the years and even wrote a poem based on a series of e-mails he exchanged with various colleagues in an effort to allow his classes the use of the library.

I'LL FIGHT YOU FOR THE LIBRARY

for Dr. Joseph D'Angelo, fifth-grade English teacher, PhD, black belt, sensei

I.

To: Clarissa Lerner, Librarian

Dear Clarissa,

I understand that the periods I reserved in the library next week for my classes have been canceled. Just out of curiosity, who and/or what is more important than my classes' research needs?

II.

To: Nancy Devlin, Secretary to Dr. Richard Blackstone, Dean of Instruction

Dear Nancy,

The librarian informs me that Dr. Blackstone has "reserved" the library for a "Facilities Utilization" meeting of the administration next week, and that all classes scheduled to meet in the library on that day must meet elsewhere. This is unconscionable. Academic instruction takes precedence over administrative meetings. Period. That Dr. Blackstone, the Dean of Instruction, would even CONSIDER canceling one class's library period in order to hold a meeting called "Facilities Utilization" is so obtuse, I am incapable of appreciating the irony in it.

III.

To: Dr. Richard Blackstone, Dean of Instruction

Dear Dick,

With all due respect, I do not think you do understand my "frustration" or else you would not have used that word. See, I am not, in fact, frustrated. The correct word would be "outraged." I will not reschedule any of my classes' library periods for any administrative meeting, especially one that purports to be discussing the effective use of the school's facilities. I do not care if the library is the only place in the school big enough to accommodate your meeting. It's also the only place in the school with books! And lastly, I would be the first to apologize for "editorializing through your secretary" if I thought the statement "Academic instruction takes precedence over administrative meetings" were a matter of opinion, and not, in fact, a matter of fact. And not one that I thought I would have to explain to the Dean of Instruction. To conclude, if any of my classes are denied the use of the school's library next week, then please alert Joyce Santiago, the District Superintendent, to be ready to accept my resignation.

IV.

To: Dr. Joyce Santiago, District Superintendent

Dear Superintendent Santiago,

For 35 years, I have served the interests of my students, providing them with all the encouragement, guidance, resources, respect and love they require to grow into productive, responsible, informed, and well-prepared members of the community. I do not take this responsibility lightly. I take it with all the nobility, grace, and gravitas of the teaching profession. So on behalf of my students and their parents, I thank you for finding another place for Dr. Blackstone to hold his meeting.

Sincerely,

Dr. Joseph D'Angelo, fifth-grade English teacher, PhD, black belt, sensei

What these three educators—Kate Millonzi, Jerome Dees, and Joseph D'Angelo—all have in common is the love and respect they had for their students. I don't know if they liked me, but they loved me; and in return, I worked hard for them. And learned more sometimes than I thought I was capable of. I grew.

THE QUEST FOR ONE THOUSAND TEACHERS

The Quest for One Thousand Teachers that I mentioned briefly in the introduction didn't come about through any kind of organized process. I did not consciously decide that I would try to inspire one thousand people to become teachers. That just started happening. (I was far too preoccupied with whether or not I would be able to make my mortgage payments after giving up my steady teaching paycheck.) People would either write to me or tell me casually in conversation that my poems about teaching—most often, specifically "What Teachers Make"—had helped them decide to enter the profession themselves. For a year, I kept a very casual mental tally and would say, "Really? I think that makes you the ninth person to tell me that." I don't know when I got the idea to start keeping track in a more organized way. But it was a journalist who told me that merely keeping track wasn't enough. It wasn't interesting. I needed a goal—and the possibility of failure. That's what would make it a story!

So I set myself a goal of one thousand new teachers and gave myself six years to reach it. And I failed miserably. By 2006, the year I was supposed to have completed the goal, the number of people I had helped convince to enter the teaching profession barely topped one hundred. But I wasn't about to give up; I liked the way having the goal had given me focus. I wasn't just a poet, I was a poet with a plan to improve the world one teacher at a time. So I decided to do away with the deadline and plot my slow and steady progress. If it took twenty-five more years to reach one thousand teachers, then so be it. Who cares if it's not a compelling story for a journalist? My real problem was that I still had no systematic and efficient way to keep track of the teachers I added to the list. I had been announcing each new convert on my blog, but that required too much e-mailing back and forth just to get all the required information from each teacher. Even after six years, it was a clunky, arduous process.

Help came in the form of a graduate student in computer programming named Jorge Casteñeda and two online interns I found on Craigslist (one of whom I didn't meet until years later) who were willing to do a lot of data entry for free. Jorge created an online form for new teachers to fill out themselves. Sarah and Airn, the interns, transferred everyone who had already signed up onto the new list. By sometime in 2007 I finally had an efficient system in place for managing the list of teachers who claimed "What Teachers Make" and my other poems had helped convince them to become teachers.

And then something happened. The word started getting out, and teachers began to sign up in greater numbers. Facebook caught on, then Twitter. As a result, every couple of months one of the videos of me performing "What Teachers Make" on You-Tube would be reposted by someone influential or placed on the front page of a website with a lot of traffic; or else some state legislature would propose another bill to balance the budget on the backs of teachers and other public sector employees, and my poem would be read at the protest like a rallying cry, which is exactly what it is. Then folks would find their way to me and my work, read about the Quest for One Thousand Teachers, and sign themselves up if they thought they met the criteria. But I also think the list started to grow for another reason: I was finally ready for it to do so.

As is so often the case, when one is ready to walk the path, the path appears. I recommitted myself to completing the Quest for One Thousand Teachers. And I added a twist . . . an extra goal: when I was done, when I had finally convinced one thousand people to become teachers, I would cut my hair, which I had been growing out since my wedding in 2006, and donate it to a program called Pantene Beautiful Lengths, which makes wigs for kids battling cancer. I would do this in memory of Tony Steinberg, the most magnanimous seventh-grader I ever taught.

TONY STEINBERG: BRAVE SEVENTH-GRADE VIKING WARRIOR

Have you ever seen a Viking ship made out of
    Popsicle sticks
and balsa wood? Coils of brown thread for ropes,
sixteen oars made out of chopsticks, and a red and
    yellow sail
made from a ripped piece of a little baby brother's
    footie pajamas?
I have.

He died with his sword in his hand and so went straight to heaven.

The Vikings often buried their bravest warriors in
ships.
Or set them adrift and on fire, a floating island of
flames,
the soul of the brave warrior rising slowly with
the smoke.
In order to understand life in Scandinavia in the
Middle Ages,
you must understand the construction of the
Viking ship.

So here's what I want the class to do:
I want you to build me a miniature Viking ship.
You have a month to complete this assignment.
You can use whatever materials you want,
but you must all work together.
Like warriors.

*These are the projects that I'm known for as a history
    teacher.*

Like the Greek Shield Project.

Or the Marshmallow Catapult Project.

Or the Medieval Castle of Chocolate Cake

(actually, that one was a disaster).

But there was the Egyptian Pyramid Project.

Have you ever seen a family of four

standing around a card table after dinner,

each one holding one triangular side

of a miniature cardboard Egyptian pyramid

until the glue finally dries?

*I haven't either, but Mrs. Steinberg said it took
    90 minutes,*

*and even with the little brother on one side
    saying,*

This is a stupid pyramid, Tony!

If I get Mr. Mali next year, my pyramid

will be designed in such a way that it will not
    necessitate
us standing here for 90 minutes while the glue
    dries!
And Tony on the other side saying,
Shut up! Shut up, you idiot!
If you let go before the glue dries
I will disembowel you with your Sony
PlayStation!
*It was the best family time they'd spent together
    since Hanukkah.*

*He died with his sword in his hand and so went
straight to heaven.*

Mr. Mali, if that's true,
that if you died with your sword in your hand
you would go straight to Valhalla,
then if you were, like, an old Viking
and you were about to die of old age,

could you keep your sword right by your bed
so if you ever felt, like, "I think I might die of
old age!"
you could reach out and grab it?

*If I were a Viking God, I don't think I would fall
for that.*
*But if I were an old Viking about to die of
old age,*
that's exactly what I would do. You're a genius.

He died with his sword in his hand and so went
straight to heaven.

*Tony Steinberg had been missing from school for
six weeks*
before we finally found out what was wrong.
*And the 12 boys left whispered the name of the
disease*
as if you could catch it from saying it too loud.

We'd been warned. The Middle School Head
    had come to class
and said Tony was coming to school on Friday.
But he's had a rough time.
The medication he's taking has made all his hair
    fall out.
So nobody stare, nobody point, nobody laugh.

I always said I liked teaching in a private school
because I could talk about God
and not be breaking the law.
And I sure talk about God a lot.
Yes, in history, of course, that's easy:
Even the Egyptian Pyramid Project
is essentially a spiritual exercise.
But how can you teach math and not believe in a God?

A God of perfect points and planes,
surrounded by right angles and archangels of
    varying degrees.

Such a God would not give cancer to a seventh-
grade boy;
wouldn't make his hair fall out from the
chemotherapy.
Totally bald in a jacket and tie on Friday
morning—
and I don't just mean Tony Steinberg—
not one single boy in my class had hair that day;
the other 12 had all shaved their heads in solidarity.
Have you ever seen 13 baldheaded seventh-grade
boys,
all pointing at each other, all staring, all laughing?

I have.

And it's a beautiful sight.
And almost as striking as 12 boys
six weeks later—now with crew cuts—
on a Saturday morning,
standing outside the synagogue

with heads bowed, holding hands
and standing in a circle
around the smoldering remains
of a miniature Viking ship,
which they have set on fire,
the soul of the brave warrior
rising slowly with the smoke.

The list that tracks the progress of the Quest for One Thousand Teachers remains at its core an entirely unscientific record. I rarely follow up with people on the list to make sure they are still teaching or that those who told me they intended to switch their major to education actually followed through and became teachers. And when I "reject" someone for being ineligible—usually because they confess they discovered my work *after* making their decision to teach—I have no way to stop them from signing up again a week later and simply omitting that confession. What can I say? I'm not a statistician.

Lastly, I should probably mention that the Quest for One Thousand Teachers is still not quite complete. As I write this at my home in New York City, I am still more than one hundred teachers short of my goal. Most likely, I'll be validating the one thousandth teacher just about the time this book is published. It will have been twelve years. Twelve years of not just writing and performing poetry about teaching, but twelve years of having a higher purpose. Part of me will be relieved to be done with the Quest for One Thousand Teachers. Part of me will enjoy having short, manageable hair again. But there will surely be another part of me that misses the feeling of working on something greater than myself. So to give myself some options in the future, I'm happy to report that I have registered the domain TenThousandTeachers.com. Just in case.

Mere parsimony is not economy. Expense, and great expense, may be an essential part in true economy.

Edmund Burke (1729–1797),
Irish-born British politician
and writer

THERE CAN
NEVER BE
A "LOST"
GENERATION

There is something that inevitably happens when discussing the challenges facing education: some people will get to a point where they want to give up on certain kinds of kids, just ignore them and focus on the ones we can help more. And I don't mean individual kids; I mean entire populations of kids, entire generations. There's a temptation to say, "Okay, we messed up with this batch. We totally failed, year after year, to give them what they needed in every aspect of their lives. And since they are now so irreparably disadvantaged, what say we cut our losses and focus on the next batch of children and promise to do better with them?"

Of course in a way many states already essentially do just this. For example, because the incidence of illiteracy in the prison population is so high, years ago Arizona started using the results of third-grade reading tests to predict the state's future prison needs. That's a horrible practice, of course, but unfortunately it seems to be remarkably accurate; if you can't read by third grade, you are more likely to end up in jail. But somewhere lost in the statistics is the ugly reality that in every state it costs at least twice as much to imprison an adult for a year as it does to educate a child. Arizona essentially says to those children who have not mastered reading by the end of third grade, "We already know what will happen to you and we are planning accordingly by devoting greater resources toward your future incarceration than we ever did to your education." How is that not giving up on a child? On a whole population of children?

On a personal level, however, face-to-face with children who have names and stories, who come to school hungry and wearing the same clothes as the day before, you cannot decide that some are no longer worth your time, no matter what the statistics seem to suggest. Teachers who tirelessly fight the good fight know this. No matter how far behind a child is, no matter how limited you think his future choices are, you cannot ever give up on him. That's what teachers make: the promise to leave every student they teach better prepared for the future than they were when they entered the class at the beginning of the year. On the most basic level, that's just what we do.

Artists and poets are the raw nerve ends of humanity. By themselves they can do little to save humanity. Without them there would be little worth saving.

Headstone in Green River Cemetery, Long Island, New York

EPILOGUE

Whatever small contribution I might have made in the writing of the poem "What Teachers Make," whether through persuading bright college graduates to consider teaching or simply by reminding veteran teachers why they chose to walk this noble path in the first place, I am well aware that it's only a drop in the bucket.

The challenges faced by teachers in the United States require and deserve much more than poetry, because the stakes are high even though the children might be small. Inequalities inherent in the public school system are resegregating our schools and widening the achievement gap between students from different socioeconomic backgrounds. Improving education in the United States is going to be maddeningly slow, bitterly contentious, and very expensive. But as they say, if you want to remind yourself of what your priorities are, look at your checkbook and see where you spend your money.

We live in times obsessed with national security, where mortgaging (and incarcerating) future generations to pay for our present security not only seems to make sense, but legitimately looks as if it is the only rational option available to us. The experts argue there is no other way. What's more, they'll say we aren't even spending enough. But that will *always* appear to be true. Whatever road you choose quickly appears to be the only road possible, the only road you can afford. It will demand greater and greater resources, over time making itself appear to be even more obviously the only option. Were someone to even suggest a different set of priorities, that person would be immediately labeled naive. So call me naive. But what if we poured trillions and trillions of dollars into the education of our children? Would we eventually come to believe that there is no other course of action available to us? That nothing else even makes sense? Would we realize we need to spend even more on improving the quality of life of future generations? Would we come to consider children the most valuable resource on earth? Because guess what? They are.

ACKNOWLEDGMENTS

First and foremost, a thank-you to Rachel Kahan, my editor at Putnam, whose idea it was for me to write this book, and to her mother, Dr. Ellen Kahan, for being a fan. Also to Alison Granuci from Blue Flower Arts for her tireless representation at all hours of the day and night. I offer my deepest thanks to the teachers who claim my work was instrumental in their decision to teach, as well as to my own teachers, colleagues, friends, and fellow itinerant poets without whom I could never have written this book, among them Nell Manning, Tim Eustis, David Stevenson, Bill Watterson, Jerome Dees, Kate Millonzi, Stewart Moss, Rick Bellamy, Larry Brown, Jorge Casteñeda, Steve Clement, Kevin Dearinger, Sarah Connell, Airn Talbert, Daniel Ferri, Jeanann Verlee, and Clark Daggett. To teachers everywhere, especially those in inner-city public schools who still actually do what I now merely write about. And lastly, to Marie-Elizabeth, a great teacher, friend, and mirror.

NOTE ON POEMS

The poems "What Teachers Make," "Totally Like Whatever, You Know?" "Like Lilly Like Wilson," and "Undivided Attention" were originally published in *What Learning Leaves* (Hanover, 2002) and are reprinted with permission.

The poems "I'll Fight You for the Library" and "Tony Steinberg: Brave Seventh-Grade Viking Warrior" were originally published in *The Last Time As We Are* (Write Bloody, 2009) and are reprinted with permission.

"I Teach for the Fire" was written for Teaching Channel and is previously unpublished.

The poem "Backwards Day," by Daniel Ferri, was originally published in *Poetry Slam: The Competitive Art of Performance Poetry*. Ed. Gary Mex Glazner. (Manic D Press, 2000). Reprinted by kind permission of the author.

ABOUT THE AUTHOR

Taylor Mali is a renowned performance poet, educator, and vocal advocate of teachers, who has performed and lectured for teachers and students all over the world. He is one of the most well-known poets to have emerged from the poetry slam movement and one of the original poets to appear on the HBO series *Def Poetry Jam*. The author of two collections of poetry, his poem "What Teachers Make" has been viewed millions of times on YouTube. He lives in New York City and performs at least one poem every Tuesday night he is in town as part of the NYC-Urbana Poetry Slam.